Joining the Dots

Also by Juliet Gardiner

Wartime: Britain 1939–1945
The Thirties: An Intimate History
The Blitz: The British Under Attack

Joining the Dots

A Woman in her Time

JULIET GARDINER

WILLIAM
COLLINS

William Collins
An imprint of HarperCollins*Publishers*
1 London Bridge Street
London SE1 9GF

www.WilliamCollinsBooks.com

First published in Great Britain by William Collins in 2017

1

ISBN 978-0-00-748916-9

Printed and bound in Great Britain by
Clays Ltd, St Ives plc

MIX
Paper from
responsible sources
FSC
www.fsc.org
FSC™ C007454

For Rudy and Sammy

Contents

Prologue

A young woman wearing a navy-blue duffel coat and bottle-green stockings stood shivering in the vaulted booking hall of Bristol Temple Meads station looking uncertainly around her. It was 1 January 1960 and the woman was me. I was sixteen years old, and, using the money I had earned from delivering letters for the Post Office during the holidays (£8 5s.) and writing 'amusing' anecdotes to the letters page of *Woman's Realm*, plus a Christmas present of a £2 postal order, I had run away from home.

It was the start of a decade that was to be momentous in changing Britain's history, politically, economically, socially and culturally. Although of course I could not have foreseen that, nevertheless it seemed a suitably significant date on which to start a new life; to leave behind the pebble-dashed house in the home counties, turn my back on the minor girls' public school and be a grown-up at last: independent, poised to achieve the freedom for which I had yearned for so long.

It was not, predictably, that simple. Progress over the next few years would be bumpy, interrupted, contradictory, frustrating. Dependencies transferred rather than jettisoned. But the world changed around me, as it did for most women in Britain – and that is the story I want to tell. It is not only or entirely my story; not a straightforward chronological account of women's history, nor a history, disquisition, celebration or critique of feminism. Rather it is a series of reflections or meditations on some of the expectations and experiences that I, like many other women in Britain, had, or could have had, during the middle years of the twentieth century.

I am a historian, and I was there, and that is what this book is about. It has no claims to be comprehensive: some important aspects of the period will be left out, or touched on only briefly; others might seem peripheral or wilfully quirky, but to me they are emblematic of various aspects of women's lives and the perception of these lives both by the women themselves and by society more generally – the education they received, the work they did; the frustrations they felt, cheek by jowl with the knowledge of widening horizons, the legislative, economic, social and intimate transformations of their lives.

It is essentially my story, the optic is mine, but to put it pretentiously, on many occasions my life could hardly fail to grind up against the arc of history, and when it did, I hope recounting that conjunction will ring true.

Chapter One

A War Baby

Although this new era started in 1960, my life began on 24 June 1943, just before the end of the Second World War.

I was a war baby born on Midsummer's Day. The previous week the RAF had mounted a major bombing raid on Düsseldorf, part of the sustained Allied attack on the Ruhr, Germany's industrial heartland. Nevertheless, the end of the war in Europe was still almost two years distant, though the tide had begun to turn. At El Alamein, Montgomery's Eighth Army had secured Britain's first military victory, defeating Rommel's Afrika Korps in November 1942. The surrender of all German troops in North Africa followed in May 1943. Alamein had led Churchill, desperate for a morale-raising British success, to venture, 'This is not the end, it is not the beginning of the end, it is, perhaps the end of the beginning.' His optimism seemed justified. By the summer of 1943 the Battle of the Atlantic was at last going the Allied way as well, with the 'killer packs' of German U-boats succeeding in sinking fewer Allied ships.

For those on the home front in Britain, however, the war remained unrelenting. Although the intense nine-month-long Blitz had ended in May 1941, frequent raids continued. One lunchtime in January 1943 a single 500kg Luftwaffe bomb was dropped on Sandhurst Road School in Catford, southeast London. Thirty-eight children and six teachers were killed in the so-called *Terrorangriff* (terror raid). There were rumours of deadly new secret weapons being developed by the Nazis. These would materialise the following summer as the lethal V1 'pilotless planes' and V2 rocket bombs. Meanwhile rationing continued, and in many cases bit deeper.

It was a courageous and optimistic decision to have a baby at this moment. Apart from the practical difficulties of shortages of baby clothes, nappies, cots, prams, feeding bottles, teats and food, there was the uncertainty of bringing a child into a world when the map to the future had been torn up into jagged pieces. No one could know how long the fighting would go on, or what form it would take.

Shock and uncertainty about the future meant that the birth rate had fallen dramatically in the early months of the war. In 1941 it had reached the lowest point since records began: 13.9 per thousand of the population. When Peggie Phillips found out that she was pregnant in June 1941, she was pleased. But her husband, John, wrote from his army camp cautioning that 'much as we would like another baby [they already had two daughters] these are hard times, and it would be wisdom to be brutal and cut off this little promise of a life until the world is a little more settled and we could find some sort of assurance that this new little person could be cared for in a decent way'.

This was the strongest argument, he suggested, 'for you going to the osteopath [an abortionist] ... Perhaps the most simple way of looking at it is that we ought to get rid of this "little accident" while it is early days yet and things haven't gone too far: and we can always have the baby at another time (if it *ever* gets to be). I hate deciding the way I have.'

Mrs Phillips took her husband's advice, raided the children's saving accounts, and on the recommendation of a doctor 'whose eyes she didn't really trust', travelled to a discreet nursing home in Kent where she paid fifty guineas for an illegal abortion. Sadly 'another time' never came, as John was killed in the battle of Monte Cassino later in the war.

Many other women had no choice but to be single mothers: they had been widowed by war. On the front page of *The Times* on the day of my birth, the list of those killed or missing in action is four times longer than the announcement of births. Some women had husbands, fiancés or boyfriends fighting abroad with no hope of home leave until the war was over.

After 1941 the birth rate rose steadily, however. Even in such an unpredictable world there were clearly many who wanted to lay down a marker for the future; to normalise the conventional progress of family life in the midst of chaos, anxiety and despair. Biological clocks ticked louder and youngest children grew older, as did their parents. War was not going to be outwitted, it had to be endured. Life, as usual, had to 'go on' and be celebrated in as many ways as possible.

Of course, as an infant I was unaware of the turbulent times into which I had been born. As I slept soundly in a second-hand Silver Cross carriage pram, under an apple tree at the end of the garden, the nation was gripped with the excitement and optimism that accompanied the news of the successful D-Day landings on 6 June 1944; I had no idea of the terror induced by the buzz bombs and V2 rockets that devastated London and parts of the home counties in the following months. Walking by the time VE Day was celebrated on 8 May 1945, I was still unlikely to have been perched in a high chair to tuck into jam sandwiches or trifle at a Victory in Europe street party. This was partly because of my young age, but also because on the whole the home counties did not go in for that kind of communal merriment.

For us there was rarely bunting and flag-waving, and we never dragged a piano into the street so that neighbours could gather round the old joanna and have a rousing sing-song. So often the most potent images of civilian war are of the urban working classes: sheltering in the Underground, emerging from their bomb-battered houses clutching all they could carry of their meagre possessions, waving Union Jacks outside Buckingham Palace or splashing in municipal fountains on VE Day. It was the working classes (some seventy per cent of the population, if assessed by the indices of unskilled or semi-skilled employment) who became the public face of the civilian war.

The middle and lower-middle classes fought a more private war. They were less likely to be found in public air-raid shelters, under archways or down the Tube. They sought protection in Anderson shelters in their own gardens or evacuated themselves as well as their children to safer places in the country or abroad. Celebrations were less exuberant and more self-contained: a glass of Bristol Cream sherry with a few close friends in the front room rather than beer or ginger pop in the street.

'The day we have waited for for nearly six years, and at last it is here, it is miraculous, exciting, wonderful,' wrote Madge Martin, the wife of an Oxford vicar, on VE Day. 'Lovely weather, streets beflagged, happy crowds dancing in the streets, singing everywhere, infectious happiness ... packed churches, thankful people.' She invited a few friends and neighbours into the vicarage, where

we listened to Churchill speak in the afternoon, quietly, no boasting. The King spoke at 9 p.m. We listened to his modest speech and drank sherry happily and rather dazedly ... before going out to see the sights ... enormous crowds shouting, cheering, dancing, huge bonfires fed by ARP properties, magnesium bombs, great logs of old chairs, tables, ladders etc. with dancing rings of young people circling them, beautiful floodlit buildings, lighted windows, torchlight processions and a good humoured gaiety with no rowdyism ... Robert [her husband] and I went about together happier than for years remembering it all for ever. Light after darkness. Thank God for this day of days.

I Don't You Know There's a Peace On?

Whatever a person's class, the dolorous grey cloud of postwar austerity hung over the whole country within days of the end of the war. The wartime excuse for shortages, regulations and bureaucratic inefficiencies – 'Don't you know there's a war on?'

– was inverted almost as soon as the VE Day celebrations were over, the bonfires damped down, the children's street parties cleared away. 'Don't you know there's a peace on?' became the ironic, resigned, sometimes bitter question in those early postwar months – one that particularly affected women. Rationing persisted until 1954 when meat was finally taken 'off the coupon', and in many cases shortages were more acute than during the war. It was estimated that housewives spent an average of at least an hour every weekday in a queue. Grocers' shelves were half empty; bread, which had never been rationed during the war, was limited to two large loaves a week of unappetising grey bread adulterated with a high chalk content and, consumers suspected, cattle feed. Strange new products were imported such as blubbery whale meat (advertised as being like steak but in fact with a fishy aftertaste) and barracuda fish, known as Snoek, that no one wanted to eat despite exhortations to mash it with chopped-up spring onions and serve it on toast, so it was eventually fed to cats, some domestic, some feral, living in roaming posses on bomb sites.

Manufacturers with nothing to sell valiantly tried to keep their brand names in the public eye for the day when they did. 'Won't it be nice when we have lovely lingerie, *and* Lux to look after our pretty things? Remember how pure, safe Lux [soap flakes] preserved the beauty of delicate fabrics?'; 'Soon all Heinz 57 varieties will be coming back into the shops, one by one'; 'Unfortunately, Cadburys are only allowed the milk to make an extremely small quantity of chocolate ... so if you are lucky enough to get some, do save it for the children ...'

The 1946 exhibition *Britain Can Make It*, staged at the Victoria and Albert Museum – the windows of which had been blown out by bomb blast, hastily replaced by requisitioning all glass production for the purpose – was designed to show that the country could again establish itself as a manufacturing nation, turning swords into ploughshares, or rather Spitfire parts into ashtrays. But though one and a half million people flocked from all over Britain to queue for a glimpse of the phoenix rising, the exhibition was soon wryly mocked as 'But Britain Can't Have It' since most British production went for export to repay the staggering debt of $3.7 billion that the country owed to the United States. As Mollie Panter-Downes, London correspondent of the *New Yorker*, wrote, 'the factories which people hoped would soon be changing over to the production of goods for the shabby, short-of-everything home consumers, are having to produce goods for export. The government will have to face up to the job of convincing the country that controls and hardships are as necessarily a part of a bankrupt peace as they were of a desperate war.'

The ambivalent adjustment to peace could be seen in the faces of the demobilised fighting men, as they exchanged their khaki or blue uniforms for ill-fitting suits. Many of the jobs they'd left when call-up papers arrived had disappeared, despite promises they would be kept open for them when they returned from the war. The workplace had changed, new skills were needed, and the colleagues who'd remained at home had overtaken them. Many women, while thankful to have husbands home again, were uneasy about having to relinquish the head-of-household role they'd been obliged to assume and to have their decisions questioned, their independence compromised. Those women who would have liked to continue to work outside the home found formidable barriers in the way: priority was given to men when it came to job vacancies; the nurseries set up during the war to enable women to work were peremptorily closed down, like theatre cloakrooms when the performance was over.

In addition, husbands often disapproved of their wives working, and a slew of childcare 'experts' pronounced on the damaging effects of maternal deprivation, insisting that mothers should remain at home, nurturing, caring. It was a measure of the largely unwelcome return to pre-war convention that women who had driven ambulances, heavy lorries and jeeps during the war were not expected to get behind the steering wheel of the family car. Fathers drove while their wives sat in the passenger seat, forced to read the map and give their husbands directions.

Both women and men came to miss the unexpected pleasures of war: the intense 'live now for today for tomorrow you may die' mentality that had led to transitory passions and fleeting, often illicit, affairs. Women yearned for the near-Hollywood glamour that one and a half million GIs from the United States had brought to Britain from 1942 until the attack on 'Fortress Europe' on D Day. They missed the catchy, energetic beat of the imported American music and the invitations to US bases where, with any luck, Glenn Miller might be leading his orchestra on the trombone. Those dances – the Lindy Hops and Jitterbug Jives – were a world away from the sedate waltzes and foxtrots of formal occasions, or the jolly, communal country dancing in village halls up and down Britain.

As the euphoria of victory flattened, diarist Madge Martin felt guilty that though she dutifully attended the harvest festival in her husband's church, she found no pleasure in the display of nature's mellow bounty.

In Barrow-in-Furness in northwest England, the middle-aged Nella Last, who had found a new confidence and purpose in her wartime work with the Women's Voluntary Service, wondered what she could do now that there was no need to raise money for the war effort, serve tea and buns to war workers, or provide clothes and comforts for the troops and refugees. Was her life to revert to looking after her uncommunicative, stick-in the-mud husband, tending her garden, and polishing the brass ornaments in her house until they gleamed?

II A Child's War

As a small child I of course had no reference point for pre-war or for the war. I missed neither white bread nor the choice of shampoos. I presumed that it was normal to carry, snail-like, an edited version of your home around with you, taking aspirins and sticking plasters in a sponge bag; cotton, needles, matches, batteries and string in an empty waxed cardboard Meltis Fruit Jellies box, in case these were unobtainable on your travels.

Hertfordshire, the county in which I was brought up, had been designated a 'neutral' area during the war, one that neither sent nor received evacuees under the official government scheme, though of course many private arrangements were made 'to get the children away' from designated danger zones.

Some stray bombs had fallen not far from my home, evidenced by craters in the roads or fields, some of which were absorbed into the landscape as ponds. By the time I was born, virtually no one carried a gas mask anymore and the Anderson shelters were gradually colonised by weeds and brambles.

I had few toys and those I had were invariably hand-me-downs from my parents and often incomplete: lead farm animals with matchsticks for legs, Dinky cars with a wheel missing. A home-made stockinet rabbit I called Tipsy was a particular companion that I pushed around in a wooden box on wheels for a pram. But I was not aware of the absence of the playthings that might have filled a middle-class child's toy cupboard in the 1930s.

There are a few reminders of war, however, that I do recall from those early postwar years. One was the evidence of destruction on trips to London, when my mother and I went shopping or visited the Wallace Collection at Hertford House, which was my mother's favourite cultural venue. She loved the domestic interiors by Dutch and Flemish artists such as Vermeer and Pieter de Hooch and found it convenient that it was just round the corner from Selfridges, and a couple of bus stops away from Daniel Neal's in Kensington for Start-rite shoes, liberty bodices, fawn knee socks and navy knickers for me.

Nothing was whole anymore, or so it seemed. Many buildings were nothing but facades; others had tarpaulins stretched and lashed down to serve as roofs; windows were boarded up, or just left as holes in the brickwork. There were sudden gaps in terraces of houses or parades of shops. Stretches of Oxford Street were like a Wild West boardwalk, and looking in the windows of John Lewis's department store which had been all but razed to the ground on 18 September 1940 was like peering into an aquarium: a narrow rectangle of glass behind which whatever paucity of merchandise was available could be glimpsed. In February 1946, *Vogue* was thrilled to report that 'Dickins & Jones [in Regent Street] are soon to have their plate-glass windows restored,' although what would be displayed in them was anyone's guess.

Rationing affected me consciously not at all. I had no pre-war abundance with which to compare the shortages, so the leather-hard liver (offal was not rationed), the tasteless mince eked out in a sea of imperfectly mashed lumpy potatoes, the slightly muddy, undersized carrots from the garden, were what I expected to be served – and was. I was unquestioning of the eggs stored in isinglass (made from fish bladder) in the larder; oblivious to the fuss made when the import of dried eggs from the US was temporarily banned; non-complicit in the illegal acquisition of butter and cream from a local farmer. It was not until sweets came 'off the coupon' in 1949, only to go straight back on again since the demand was so heavy it could not be satisfied, that rationing impacted on me. I had spotted something I liked and pointed to it, only to discover that chewing gum was not the nougat I had imagined it to be.

The other subtler memory is of class, which I could neither conceptualise nor name as such at the time. I recall very well the gossip that I would later recognise as disquiet that *class*, and thus power relations, had been turned upside down during the war – and the implacable determination to set them to rights again. In my mother's view – and she was not alone in this –

shopkeepers had become very 'uppity', reserving special goods on points, keeping the occasional few oranges under the counter for favoured customers. Such retailers seemed to regard the long queues that formed outside shops as their personal supplicants. The grocer who weighed out sugar in blue paper bags, scooped biscuits from glass-topped tins, sent his delivery boy round weekly on his bicycle with my mother's order of rashers of streaky bacon and a box of Post Toasties cereal, must have realised that as ration books disappeared, his control was ebbing. The customer was again king (or rather queen) and had a choice of shops to patronise. The half-crown or capitalist ten-shilling note became the only currency of exchange required, instead of the government-issued ration book to be stamped.

Herbie Gates was one of the church wardens at St Mary's Church, Hemel Hempstead, where my mother went to matins every Sunday and was a member of the Mothers' Union. Before the war he had sometimes helped with the heavy work in our garden, but during the war he had volunteered for Civil Defence duties, becoming an ARP warden, a responsibility he had taken very seriously, even officiously. 'Little 'itler' was murmured as he admonished *Put out that light!* to householders demonstrating inadequately observed blackout. Now that he had handed back his brassard and tin hat, he too must be cut down to size, according to my mother and her neighbours, and put to setting potatoes, scything nettles and taking the church collection plate again, rather than having his wartime authority recognised as was surely his due.

It is not surprising that I have no memory of the war or its immediate aftermath, but what is surprising is that while I could read the signifiers of shortages and destruction, I had almost no factual knowledge until I was almost an adult about this cataclysmic event that would slice the twentieth century in two. No one I knew wanted to talk about the war that had gone on too long and too painfully and had put lives on hold for half a generation. There was no narrative of the war, though it was proffered as an explanation for many things, including the appearance one Sunday lunchtime of a neighbour who had been in a Japanese POW camp for three years, crawling on his stomach through the open French windows of his family home some months after his release, a knife clenched between his teeth as he threatened his wife and children.

Boys played cowboys and Indians, not Tommies and Nazis; we looked at maps of the British Empire in primary school, not the world at war. The Second World War was not on the syllabus at secondary school either, and nor was it offered as a topic when, much later, I went to read history at university.

There were soon plenty of books about the military aspects of war: battles, generals' memoirs, discussions of causes, strategies and hardware. Cinema-goers too thrilled in time to such heroic films as *The Wooden Horse* and *The Dam Busters*. But the civilian experience remained largely unspoken. During the war, films such as *Waterloo Road*, *Millions Like Us*, *Went the Day Well?* and *Mrs Miniver* had filled cinemas with their subtle – and sometimes not so subtle – messages of propaganda and encouragement for the home front. Give your all for the war effort; pull together for victory; keep faithful and devote your energies to keeping your home happy and secure for when your fighting man returns. Immediately after the war, the dreariness of wartime sacrifice was not what cinema-goers wanted to be reminded of; the films they flocked to see were comedies, musicals, historical dramas and thrillers.

Richard Titmuss's volume of the official history of the civilian war, *Problems of Social Policy*, came out in 1950 but it was not until the late 1960s that books for the general reader began to be published. Angus Calder's *The People's War*, the first – and to date the best – book on the civilian war in Britain, much influenced by Titmuss, was published in 1969, followed in 1971 by Norman Longmate's history of everyday life in wartime Britain, *How We Lived Then*. The first of the twenty-six episodes of the epic series *The World at War* directed by Jeremy Isaacs was shown on ITV in October 1973. 'Home Fires Burning: Britain', the single episode on the civilian side of the war, written by Angus Calder, was transmitted on 13 February 1974.

There were many hard-working and courageous women who joined the forces in the war and gradually the great value of the Auxiliary Territorial Service (ATS), the Women's Royal Naval Service (WRNS), the First Aid Nursing Yeomanry (FANYs) and the Women's Auxiliary Air Force (WAAFs) was recognised, as was the story of the heroic women recruits to the SOE (Special Operations Executive). However, the contribution of women on the home front was slower to be acknowledged. This was in no way solely a women's domain: think firefighters, Civil Defence and Observer Corps, medical staff and many more organisations which in most cases consisted of more men than women. Nonetheless, women did 'keep the home fires burning', in their own houses if their meagre coal rations stretched to it, but also on the land, in banks and offices, in munitions and aircraft factories, on buses, in postal services, as porters at railway stations, and in welfare and medical services.

Statues of Second World War generals and leaders strut on plinths throughout the country. Even the animals – horses, dogs, pigeons, mules – who served in various ways in wars had a monument erected at the edge of Hyde Park in 2004. But it was not until nearly a year later that a sombre bronze monument depicting the wartime uniforms women had worn, both military and civilian, hanging, discarded, from hooks, was unveiled in Whitehall close to the Cenotaph. Certainly I had no idea in those early postwar years of the professionalism and heroism that must have been displayed by the women around me. It was many years later, through my work as a historian, that I came to understand the texture of the time.

Chapter Two

Second-Hand Baby

The sun was shining in through the net curtains, making laser-pointed parallel shafts of dust in the late summer light as I sat on the gloss-painted windowsill in the dining room, looking through a large Marshall & Snelgrove dress box full of photographs. I had been given a photograph album and a small packet of photo corners for my eighth birthday in June 1951, and on this September afternoon, the last day of the school holidays, I was sorting through the photos to choose which I wanted to stick into the album, to create a storyboard of my life so far.

There were pictures of me aged about two, perhaps, sitting on the grass wearing a sun bonnet; one of me with a terrified-looking friend, crouching naked in a tin bath on the lawn as an unseen hand aimed a water jet from a hosepipe at us. There were also a number of photographs taken on the promenade in Paignton, Devon. One showed me sitting on a moth-eaten stuffed horse on the seafront; another with my cousin Sheila, who usually came on holiday with us so that I had someone to play with, eating candy floss on the same promenade. We always spent a fortnight there in August, staying in a boarding house owned by a Mrs Pollard, overflowing with souvenirs from various other seaside resorts she had visited. Once a week she would urge us to hurry back from the beach as there was chicken for dinner that night (in those days chicken was a rare delicacy).

Then in the box I found a sheet of Polyfotos, each the size of a passport photograph, printed like a cine film so that each sequential frame showed a slight variation from the one before and the one after. A lurking smile might be replaced by a full-on grin; a blurred, waving hand give way to a face half turned from the camera. This was a record designed to animate the subject in a way that the frozen image of a single shot never could.

But at the bottom of the box I encountered a photograph I could not recall having seen before – of a baby I did not recognise lying on a shawl. The rest of the sepia or black-and-white photos in this repository of my parents' recorded life had some sort of identification pencilled on the back – 'Chas. and Dolly's wedding, 18 June 1927', 'Picnic with Hilda and Bill, Swanage, August 1951', 'Giddy [with a hard 'G', my infant attempt at the name I went by then, Gillian] feeding ponies on Dartmoor, August 1950'. However, the photograph of the baby had no identification. The back was covered with what was known as butterfly tape, a wide band of gummy white paper which, when licked, would stick to paper or card. Curious to know who the baby was, I carefully started to peel the paper off. 'This is my baby for adoption. Her name is Olivia. Weight at birth 6lb 4ozs.' I knew then who the baby was. Me.

For dramatic effect, I wish I could say that this was the first time I had known that I was adopted, but that would not be true. And so many half-truths, evasions and downright fantasies accrue round the identity of an adopted child that it seems important to nail the few incontestable facts.

I Adoption

Until the 1920s, the adoption of babies and children had been a casual, informal affair with no legal process involved. It was not until 1943 that it became compulsory to register adoptions. Children were regarded much as chattels: the responsibility but also the property of those who had created them. The babies of unmarried mothers might well be absorbed into the family, the mother stripped of her maternal status and passed off as an older sister or an aunt. Or a baby might be handed on like one of a litter of puppies or kittens in excess of requirements, to a more distant relation, friend or neighbour who didn't have children of her own and wanted a baby, or to a motherly soul who already had such a large brood that one more wouldn't make much difference.

The writer Ian McEwan's mother handed her baby over at Reading station to a couple who had answered a newspaper advert. Later she bore two more children, one of them Ian. And in 1938 the mother of the future children's author Allan Ahlberg, carrying a string bag containing bootees, a baby's bottle and a shawl, had travelled from Paddington to an orphanage in Battersea where she 'signed a couple of documents', the infant Allan was handed over to her and she returned to

Paddington where her husband was waiting, clutching 'her secret/ On her lap/ From all the other passengers/ All the way back', and the new family caught another train home to Oldbury in the Black Country.

Many of these informal arrangements probably worked out reasonably satisfactorily for the child and its new family, but there were sensational reports in the newspapers from time to time about 'baby farming', when a usually middle-aged woman who had advertised in a local newspaper offering to provide a home for a baby for a cash payment, was subsequently found to have starved, neglected, beaten or even killed babies in her care. The most notorious case was that of Mrs Amelia Dyer of Reading who was hanged in 1896 after being convicted largely on the evidence of her daughter of strangling a baby and dumping its body in the Thames. The police estimated that Mrs Dyer had done away with at least twenty and possibly as many as 200 babies that had been entrusted to her care by their mothers.

Throughout my childhood, a wax model of the fearsome-looking Mrs Dyer standing in the dock of the Old Bailey could be seen in the Chamber of Horrors in Madame Tussauds on the Marylebone Road in London. It terrified yet compelled me, and lying in bed at night I would conjure up that monstrous black-clad figure with prominent teeth and a cold, sightless gaze. This would alternate in my imagination with G. F. Watts's melancholy painting *Hope* (1886), a large reproduction of which hung in our hallway at home. This gloomy allegorical depiction of a blind woman sitting on a globe, her eyes bandaged as she strains to hear the faint music of the broken lyre she is holding, haunted me for years, and I am at one with G. K. Chesterton who wrote that a more appropriate title would have been 'Despair'. To me these were the two most frightening images possible, and their nightly evocation, I imagined, would be a talisman; the equivalent of a lucky rabbit's paw, which would somehow keep the dark forces of night at bay.

The desperate plight of an unmarried mother and her intense desire for secrecy would mean she was in no position to enquire too closely into the circumstances of the person to whom she was handing over her infant, and there were no legal requirements on either side, just an implicit understanding that the mother would not seek to reclaim the baby she had effectively sold, nor the 'adopter' seek to return it. The drawbacks to this casual exchange were addressed to a small extent in the first Infant Life Protection Act of 1872, which required that anyone receiving two or more infants under the age of one (eventually raised to seven by the Children's Act of 1908) for 'hire or reward' was obliged to register her address with her local authority, or in the case of London, with the Metropolitan Board of Works. But these safeguards were neither effective nor enforced.

Concern sharpened after the First World War when there was a positive glut of babies in need of care, either orphans, the progeny of widows whose husbands had been killed fighting, or babies born out of wedlock. Around 42,000 of them – 'children of the mist' – were in this last category at the war's end. This figure was not reached again until the year of my birth, towards the end of the Second World War, when the rate of illegitimate births leapt from 36,000 in 1942 to 43,000 the following year.

However, moves to regulate adoption practices in the inter-war years came not from the government but from voluntary organisations, following the example of Clara Andrews whose work in Exeter with child refugees from Belgium during the First World War had convinced her that there was a need for some sort of a broker between unwanted children and would-be parents. The National Children's Adoption Association (NCAA) was intended to do just that: those wishing to adopt a child were given full details of the child's background and medical history, while a certificate of health and references were required both from the child's parents and from the putative adopter, and similar procedures were also the practice for Dr Barnardo's and other charities which arranged for the permanent placement of 'unwanted' children with families, or very occasionally with single women.

Nevertheless, throughout the interwar period adoption was regarded as a last resort, even in the case of the unmarried mother. It was argued that all should be done to help her keep her child rather than have it adopted. The National Council for the Unmarried Mother and her Child, set up in 1918, insisted that this was generally the best solution and that more support should be given to the mother to enable her to keep her child. This view was influenced by a belief in the strong biological bond between a birth mother and her child, and by a concern that potential adopters could be impulsive and sentimental in their desire for a child and might not have fully thought through the responsibilities and stresses of parenthood. If a young woman could just hand over her baby for adoption and thus relieve herself of any responsibility for it, it was deemed likely that she would not learn her lesson and moral turpitude would go unchecked. Moreover, many eugenicists considered that personality traits were genetic and likely to be inherited: they would 'out' like physical characteristics such as blue eyes or blond hair. So an infant born out of wedlock was seen as preordained to have a not entirely reliable moral compass: as clear as an unsightly birth mark, an irremovable moral stain tainted the innocent bastard.

Most people looking to adopt wanted a no-strings orphan of two or three years old, whereas in fact most children on offer were illegitimate and most of these were babies. In her book on adoption (*A Child for Keeps*), Jenny Keating explains the preference at this time for a toddler rather than a newborn as proof that the child came from sufficiently good stock to survive infancy, since its genetics, its inborn nature, would be the defining characteristic in its development. Subsequently, with more awareness of psychoanalytic theories' emphasis on the dominance of nurture over nature, potential adopters were more attracted to the idea of a newborn infant as being a tabula rasa on whom they could imprint their own ideas and values.

Indeed, over the course of the twentieth century, the notion of intuitive mothering was increasingly challenged by the popularity of manuals from a growing number of experts in both child health and child psychology. From Truby King, with his belief in fresh air and rigidly regulated feeding and cuddling routines, to the altogether more relaxed and more permissive Dr Benjamin Spock, who encouraged mothers to trust their babies' instincts, or on to the middle-way Penelope Leach or the draconian, childless Gina Ford, the zeitgeist of the nursery had changed. Mothering was not purely instinctive: it could be learned, it had a scientific, research-based dimension. The effect of this could hardly fail to narrow the gap between the 'natural' or birth mother and the adoptive mother, since both could be seen clutching the same latest fashionable mothering manual, both as perplexed by questions of babies sleeping on their back or front, of yes or no to dummies, the right age to potty-train, how to deal with the tantrums of the 'terrible twos'.

A newborn baby being brought home from hospital was also a simulacrum of the natural arrival of an infant, its provenance obscured in the soft folds of the lacy white shawl in which it was likely to be enveloped. This was apparently particularly pleasing to middle-class adopters, for whom the unpleasant miasma of the 'baby farm' still obstinately tended to cling to the idea of adoption. In any case, the appearance of a toddler in the household of a childless couple announced in a starkly obvious way their failure, with no IVF or other aids to fertility available, to produce a child in the time-honoured way, whereas the arrival of a newborn baby was a more ambiguous event. If the arrival of a child signalled a 'normal family', why would adoptive parents wish to disrupt that conventionality if they could avoid it by proclaiming to the world that their family was 'different', their child a foundling of uncertain pedigree?

II Arrival

Given my age, I did not, of course, arrive at my new home wrapped in a shawl but, I was told – though I have been unable to find any photographic corroboration – dressed in a tweed coat with a velvet collar, tweed bonnet and tweed leggings (which were not like today's leggings but more like trousers with elastic that went under the shoe). I was, I think, about two and a half years old, the paperwork required by the 1926 Adoption of Children Act completed, and only a short court hearing in front of a magistrate still to come, followed by the issue of a shortened birth certificate. This was half the size of a usual one and with no space for the name, occupation or parish of either parent, but was nevertheless a legal document of irrevocable status that gave an adopted child the same rights and legal status as a natural-born one when it came to inheritance. It was a 'fresh start', 'a new page' in my life. And stark evidence for evermore that I had been adopted.

I was illegitimate, as were more than 40,000 babies born during or just after the Second World War. I was adopted from the Church of England Incorporated Society for Providing Homes for Waifs and Strays (subsequently the Dickensian evocation of Waifs and Strays was dropped in favour of the simple 'Children's Society'), where I'd been placed when I was probably about two months old after the original adoption arrangements made at birth had fallen through, since a severe case of bronchitis suggested that I might have a congenital chest condition and thus could not be granted the clean bill of health required for the adoption to go ahead. I believe it is the same with cows: they have to be certified fit before they can leave the cattle market for new byres.

A warning here. 'All Cretans are liars,' said the Cretan. 'All adoptees are fantasists,' said the adoptee. Certainly I am; a natural spinner of a skewed family romance. I not only exist in a personal historical void, I *am* a void, officially a *filius nullius*. I have no given past, no known sidebars. I am obliged to answer 'I don't know, I am adopted', when asked if there is a history of diabetes, or high blood pressure, or insanity, in my family. Thus, it seems not unreasonable that given a blank sheet of paper, a true tabula rasa, one is unable to distinguish, or chooses not to distinguish, fact from fiction in the narrative of one's life. I fill in the void, inscribing the abyss in ways that make my free-floating self seem more interesting, more desirable, by the construction of grander birth parents and more intriguing circumstances surrounding my birth. If I am rootless, why not sink my roots in the richest, most friable soil possible?

I sometimes say now that I am not entirely sure what the truth about me is, and that at least is true, but that is because over the decades, my memories and fantasies about my memories have calcified with what little I have been told, and that edifice is now the truth and I have no certain way of dismantling it. I may even occasionally find myself adding another layer or smear of obfuscation.

Under the terms of the 1926 Adoption Act, adoption had been intended to be an open process; the adopters' names and addresses appeared on the consent form the parents (or more likely the mother) who gave a child up for adoption signed to enable this. But this transparency could prove to be an inhibition to would-be adopters who wanted the child they had adopted to be considered to be theirs, just as a birth child was. They were not prepared to trade the ambiguity of their family's formation for legal regulation. They preferred their unregulated parental status to taking the possible consequences when not only the adopted child, but the world at large, could know the truth. This was considered particularly true of 'villadom', presumably the lower middle classes who guarded their privacy fiercely from neighbours 'poking their noses into other people's business'. But some working-class parents stated that they had chosen to move to another town to obscure the knowledge of their status as adoptive parents, whilst 'some hunting people' (presumably upper-class) admitted that 'if we had to go into court, even a magistrate's room to have this legalised, we would not do it. We would give up the child rather than that it should be known that it came through a society.'

This blotting-out of an adopted child's origins was concret-ised by the 1949 Adoption Act, which raised a high wall of secrecy. It decreed that the birth mother would not in future be informed of the name of her child's adoptive parents nor where they lived: in future, only a serial number would appear on the adoption papers, in place of the previously uncoded informa-tion. The sponsor of the bill in the Lords, Viscount Simon, insisted that 'it was in the interest of the child that the birth mother should not haunt the home of the new family'. An iron curtain was to be dropped between the natural and adoptive parent so that it would be extremely difficult for a mother to trace the child she had relinquished.

However, despite this officially erected fence, it was increas-ingly accepted that it was unrealistic to imagine such an intim-ate secret could be kept in perpetuity. Furthermore, it would be traumatic for a young person to find out, perhaps at puberty, that the people he or she had regarded as its 'natural parents' were in fact not biological relations. The rock on which the young person's identity had been grounded could crumble; they would be most likely to feel vulnerable, deceived and betrayed in the most fundamental manner. What else in their young lives was not true? Where did veracity lie, if not with the person they believed had borne them? To avoid this trauma of exposure, agencies strongly advised parents that their children should be told that they were adopted as soon as they were able to comprehend what that meant – somewhere between three and six years was reckoned to be optimum.

I can't remember when I was told that I was adopted, but I must have been quite young. However, once this information had been imparted, it was never referred to again and I was discouraged from asking more or alluding to the fact. Once, after being bought a doll in a toyshop, I remarked, 'She's adopted like me', and was hustled out of the shop by my mother who said sharply: 'We don't talk about that.'

If I ever asked who my birth mother was, my adoptive mother would reply: 'You don't need to know that. You are ours now.' This seems reasonable since in the immediate postwar world 'birth mother' was not a phrase in common currency, rather it would have been 'real mother', which must have been immensely hurtful to a woman who had done everything for the child short of pushing her out into the world. Who was the 'real' mother in this context? The bearer or the carer?

I understood, and I was prepared to believe – I think – that I was more special because I had been specifically chosen; rather than just slithering into my mother's life with no chance of return or refund. I was told that I had been picked out because

I had blue eyes and a nice smile – and in any case two-thirds of those wishing to adopt expressed a preference for a girl.

But what I did find very hurtful for many years were the veiled allusions, the snide remarks – 'I'm afraid that you are fast growing up to be like your [birth] mother' – with no more insight as to what that meant and why it was something I should not want to happen. And worst of all was my mother's occasional taunt of 'If only you knew who your father was ...', and no matter how much I begged to be told, my mother's lips would purse into a stony silence leaving me none the wiser as to whether he might have been the Duke of Windsor, General Montgomery, or an American GI 'over here' to prepare for D Day (as I often fantasised).

My adoption was not terribly successful. My mother and I were a disappointment to each other. I was not the daughter she had hoped for, nor she the mother I would have chosen if such a reversal of choice had been on offer. She was, like so many mid-century women, I suspect, disappointed by life. She was of working-class origin but had a burning desire to be middle-class, with all the attributes and appurtenances that implied. Her father had been a railwayman, a signal keeper, I think, living in Walton, near Peterborough, who was dead before I came into the lives of Mr and Mrs Wells. Her mother, of whom she had been very fond, was also dead. My maternal grandmother had been nursed by her in our house in her dying months, though I cannot reliably remember her. I suspect that my mother was deeply saddened that she seemed unable to recreate with me the mother–daughter bond she'd had with her own mother.

My mother (Dorothy Fanny – known as Dolly – whose second name never ceased to make my children laugh) had wanted to be an infant school teacher, but that was an aspiration too far for a working-class girl in the aftermath of the First World War, educated only to the age of thirteen at an elementary school. I am not sure what she did for a living before she married; she was always very cagey about that, but I suspect that she was in service. Not in a grand Downton Abbey sort of a house with its life below stairs, its 'pug's parlour', its ladies' maids, its grooms and butler, but rather as a 'cook general', that loneliest of lives, the sole servant in a middle-class suburban villa, 'doing' for two bachelor businessmen, cleaning, shopping, cooking plain meals, washing and ironing. A housewife in all respects but those that one might think had meaning.

Things had brightened for her when she met my father, Charles, who was just a rung above her in her carefully calibrated social ladder. He had the ambition to be a doctor, but before he achieved medical school his father, a heavy drinker and, I suspect, a wife-beater, had died and that put paid to his ambition, since his wages were needed to help the family's meagre income. My parents married in 1927, she in a drop-waisted, flapper-style cream silk dress and narrow satin T-bar shoes. A similar miniature shoe in silver, filled with wax orange blossom, and a silver cardboard horseshoe topped their wedding cake. My parents kept this souvenir, together with a collection of heraldic Goss china and a glass tube filled with layers of different-coloured sand (from Alum Bay in the Isle of Wight, where they had spent their honeymoon), in a glass-fronted display cabinet in the dining room throughout my childhood.

After their wedding, my parents set up home in privately rented accommodation (as most people did in the late 1920s) near Watford in Hertfordshire, moving a few miles to Hemel Hempstead when my father got a job in the local Borough Surveyor's department. Eventually he would build – or customise the plans of a spec builder – the house in which they would live for some forty-five years. So in the mid-1930s my parents became proud home owners (or rather mortgage holders) of a pebble-dashed detached house with a rectangular garden back and front.

It was some time before they got round to starting the process of adoption. When I once asked my mother why she hadn't had a child, she replied that the egg 'kept coming away', by which I presume she meant that she had had a series of miscarriages. Maybe hope ran out in the early days of the war. Maybe my father needed persuading – though I doubt that. Maybe the vicar had suggested it as a distraction from the nervous headaches my mother suffered from and a Christian gesture towards a cast-out child. They were quite old – in their late forties, which seemed much older then than it does now – to embark on first-time parenthood with a young child. And they were – unsurprisingly – stuck in their ways, rigid in their routines, unused to the noise and tumbling of childhood. 'Steady, steady', was the admonition most heard in our house, according to the recollection of childhood friends invited to tea.

I was frequently reminded that I was lucky to have been adopted, otherwise I would have ended up in an orphanage, or a children's home. After all there were so many illegitimate babies on offer at the end of the Second World War – a regular 'baby scoop' the Americans called it. The uncertainty, danger, intensity and impermanence of wartime was conducive to unlikely liaisons and fleeting couplings, since men and women moved around more in wartime, posted away from their home surroundings to places where they knew no one and sought comfort or adventure. Some babies were born to single women, others to wives who'd had an affair while their husbands had been away fighting abroad or working elsewhere in war production. In some cases, the returning husband was prepared to forgive his wife's 'lapse' on condition that the consequence was adopted. However, the novelist Barbara Cartland, who had advised WAAFs on welfare and personal problems during the war and turned to counselling returning war veterans after the war, advised men to try to accept this situation. 'At first they swore that as soon as it was born the baby would have to be adopted, but then sometimes they would say, half shamefaced at their generosity, "the poor little devil can't help itself, and after all it's one of hers".'

As I grew up I did indeed regard myself as fortunate to have been adopted. It sounds an unkind, and certainly an ungrateful thing to say, but I came to rejoice in my status as an adopted child. I was not 'one of them', I realised as I grew up. The traits that I found difficult or irritating about my mother were characteristic of *her*, not part of *my* make-up. I was a superior being, I conjectured, since I had no evidence; certainly the child of a very clever and beautiful mother, in the temporary custody of some rather banal earthlings. I did not expect to be reclaimed by this exotic yet warmly maternal creature, but this belief would eventually give me the confidence to strike out a new route to fulfilment and happiness, far from the high laurel hedges, Rexine furniture and conversations that invariably failed to move beyond remarks about the weather or comments on the food: 'This lamb's not as tender as last Sunday's joint, Dolly.' All I had to do was bide my time. Which is essentially what I did throughout my childhood and school years, waiting, confident that being grown up would change everything.

Despite a more relaxed attitude towards the 'accidents' of wartime, opinions hardened again during the postwar years of dreary austerity. Throughout the 1950s and into the 1960s, the 'shame' of illegitimacy still persisted, with the fear of a missed period blighting many young girls' lives. Middle-class pregnant daughters were invariably sent by private arrangement to mother and baby homes, usually in the country but certainly far from their own neighbourhoods. There, they would give birth, and the baby would usually be taken for adoption, sometimes against the wishes of the mother, who would return to her family home and her old life after 'a holiday with relatives' or 'a temporary job abroad'. She would slip back into her former life as if nothing had happened. But it had, of course. Regardless of how much she accepted that this was the only realistic course, the bereft mother had suffered a profound loss, and many women found themselves forever unable to forget the babies they had carried for nine months, given birth to, nursed for weeks, only to have the infant taken away.

For those without such resources, relatives or charitable institutions were called upon. 'Being pregnant and unmarried in 1950 was something you wouldn't wish on your worst enemy,' wrote Sheila Tofield, who worked in the typing pool of the

National Assistance Board in Rotherham. To her surprise and horror, she recalled in her 2013 memoir *The Unmarried Mother*, she found she was pregnant after sleeping with a former colleague who washed his hands of any responsibility. 'If people did something that went against the social norm in those days, no one sympathised or tried to understand. It was simple: there were "nice girls" and there was the other sort, who brought shame on themselves and their families. And that was the sort of girl I had now become.' Sheila Tofield's brother effectively disowned her, while her mother was apoplectic at the 'disgrace' she had brought on her family. Her response was to half fill a tin bath with boiling water, command her daughter to climb in, and hand her a quarter-bottle of gin, instructing her to 'drink this and then go to bed'.

When this abortion attempt proved unsuccessful, Miss Tofield wrote to Evelyn Home, the 'agony aunt' at the magazine *Woman*, explaining that she was unmarried and pregnant and her mother was adamant that she could not keep the baby and it would have to be adopted. The reply was the standard one: she should get in touch with an organisation run by the Church of England, in this case in Sheffield. The woman who interviewed her told Sheila that she would be sent to a mother and baby home in Huddersfield:

'You'll go there for six weeks before your due date and remain there for six weeks after the birth. When the baby's born, you'll take care of it until it's adopted.' She didn't give me any details of what she called 'the adoption process' or anything about how the people who would become the parents of my child would be selected. And I didn't ask. I knew that what I had done was 'wrong' and I didn't expect sympathy or kindness from anyone, or to be offered a choice about anything. I was just thankful there was somewhere I could go to have the baby before I went home again and tried to pretend that none of it had ever happened.

So on the morning of the day she had hoped would never come, Sheila Tofield packed a small case and caught two buses to Huddersfield. 'I was setting out on a journey I didn't want to make, to a town I didn't want to go to, where I'd do something I didn't want to do.'

It was not until the more permissive 1960s that the stigma of illegitimacy began to ebb, and a decisive moment came in 1975 when transparency triumphed. Legislation made it possible for an adoptee to obtain a copy of his or her full birth certificate from the General Register Office; this gave the name and address of the birth mother, and her occupation at the time of her child's birth, but in the case of unmarried parents, not of the father unless he chose to be named.

I have never tried to track down my birth mother, though over the years I have gleaned from an aunt who thought I deserved some (but not much) information about my identity the fact that she was Italian – probably from northern Italy. Whether she was a student over here when war broke out and elected to stay, or was interned in 1940 after the fall of France when Mussolini joined the Axis powers (unlikely but not impossible), or whether she was of Italian extraction but her family had lived in Britain for at least a generation, I don't know.

When I was a young child I think I was wise enough to realise that this glamorous, brilliant mother I had conjured up was most likely to be an illusion. After all, my friends' and neighbours' mothers were much like my own, with their greying, tightly permed hair, felt hats, slightly shabby clothes and sensible shoes. (Clothes only ceased to be rationed in 1949 and the wartime 'make do and mend' ethos was still prevalent among British women.)

As I grew up, I felt I had no need for another mother, since the one I had already had proved less than satisfactory in my view. Soon I had a husband and children of my own and I could not imagine where a spare additional mother would fit into the family structure. Later still I realised that I didn't want to learn that my mother had been felled by a fearsome hereditary disease that I was likely to develop, or that she was still alive and had some form of senile dementia that would leave me, despite her abrogation of me, somehow bound to take responsibility for her.

So for these semi-rational reasons, which no doubt hide a deeper, more profound anxiety, I have never tried to find my mother. I was (and still am) more interested in finding out who my father was, but that would be a much harder task since his name does not appear on my birth certificate. Maybe I will someday follow that path to discovery, if time is allowed to me, if only for my children and grandchildren's sake. They have the right not to have a central branch of their already woefully sparse family tree amputated.

Chapter Three

An Education (of Sorts)

My first memory of my education is a Freudian one. I was standing next to a little boy on my first day at what was grandly
called 'nursery school' but was a corner of the dining room in a
neighbour's house. There was a toy cash register, some Meccano,
a doll's pram accommodating a doll and a dog-eared teddy bear
with a tea towel as a coverlet, and a sandpit in the garden,
covered by a tarpaulin which was rolled back in the summer to
allow 'messy play' with buckets and spades and child-sized
watering cans. Perhaps there was a roll of blue sugar paper and
wax crayons or poster paints to make pictures with, and blunt
scissors and squares of coloured sticky paper too, but I don't
remember.

What I do remember was the willy this little boy fished out
of his shorts and directed at the lavatory (or toilet as I was
instructed to call it) as a stream of wee arced precisely where it
was intended to go. I felt sheer, gut-wrenching penis envy –
the functionality, the utility, a body part with the same

straightforward application as a garden hose, no more lifting up
skirts, pulling down knickers, balancing precariously on cold
porcelain rims. I wanted what he had and carefully checked and
rechecked my anatomy to see if somewhere I too had such a tap.
I had no idea if this was a usual male adjunct, or if this particular
child had been singularly blessed – or maybe adapted? And as
far as I remember, I never asked, just coveted.

I One Potato, Two Potatoes . . .

The postwar government had other educational priorities so,
largely for financial reasons but also in the belief that very
young children were best at home with their mothers, it
discouraged local authorities from investing in pre-school
education when so many resources were needed for the provision of secondary schooling following the 1944 Education Act.
Indeed, as late as the 1960s, the percentage of children attending nursery schools had barely increased since the 1930s, and
where this was provided it was usually as a result of local
authority subsidies for underprivileged areas. My nursery was a
private one, paid for weekly, I imagine, with a charge that
included a mid-morning beaker of milk and a biscuit. It would
be pressure from married women wanting to go back to work
in the 1960s and 70s that finally led the government to develop
systematic pre-school provision for the children of any parent
who wanted to make use of it.

Since I was an only child with no cohabiting playmates, I was
fortunate to be able to spend time with a handful of other children of my age, learning to share, make friends, play with

bricks, sing 'Old MacDonald Had a Farm' and 'Ten Green Bottles', and to write my name in higgledy-piggledy capitals.

After a year or so at nursery it was time to go to 'proper school', so I was sent to George Street primary, a former board school, just down the hill from where we lived. It was a grim place with high windows so children could not be distracted by what was going on outside. The lavatories were in the far corner of the yard. They were fitted with doors that didn't close properly so you somehow had to stretch one leg from where you were sitting to keep the door shut while naughty boys tried to get in. There was an asphalt playground back and front with an inevitable tendency to graze knees, yet with no play equipment; games at playtime consisted of chalking hopscotch squares on the ground or playing fives with pebbles. The girls walked round and round the playground, arms intertwined, or skipped, tucking their dresses into their knickers and chanting 'One potato, two potatoes, three potatoes, four' as they jumped over the turning rope held by two friends.

As I grew older I considered the home counties a dull and unenviable place to grow up. It had no distinctive regional culture, traditions or dialect. It was neither urban nor rural, but a commuter land full of dormitory towns where people came home and tended their gardens or did a little light woodwork in their refuge shed after the train had dropped them off from London at about six o'clock. My father worked locally and so walked home for dinner (lunch) and then came home to high tea, which I remember as a meal of ham, hard-boiled eggs, lettuce and a lot of beetroot, though the repast must have varied sometimes.

You could plot the days of the week by the meals we ate: roast meat on Sunday, the remains of the joint on Monday, shepherd's pie on Tuesday, with the last stringy remains of Sunday's meal minced, macaroni cheese on Wednesday, liver and onions (ugh) on Thursday, fish on Friday. Puddings were things like plum pies, treacle tart, suet pudding and Bird's Instant Whip, which my mother claimed was 'home made' as she added milk to the strawberry, banana or caramel packet powders.

Hemel Hempstead, where I grew up, was a smallish Hertfordshire market town and did not become suburbanised in the first wave of suburb-building. Mostly the town was not part of the 1930s growth of home ownership away from the crowded and fetid capital. No ring roads emanated from its core, though it was obviously ripe for change, given the post-war planning movement to settle families around the circumference of London and other overcrowded industrial towns and cities, but it would always lack any distinction as far as I was concerned.

This perception was confirmed when I read Iona and Peter Opie's collection of the rhymes children chanted as they skipped, published in 1959 when my skipping days were not long past, and noted fascinating topical, regional and local references. In Lancashire the Opies heard girls chime, to the tune of 'Red Sails in the Sunset', a rhyme about a GP in Lancaster who had been hanged in 1936 for the murder of his wife and the girl who looked after the children:

Red stains on the carpet, red stains on your knife

Oh Dr Buck Ruxton, you murdered your wife,

The nursemaid she saw you, and threatened to tell,

Oh Dr Ruxton, you killed her as well,

as they skipped. In 1952 in Hackney, the Opies reported hearing children chanting in a primary school playground:

We are three spivs of Trafalgar Square,

Flogging nylons, tuppence a pair

All fully fashioned, all off the ration,

Sold in Trafalgar Square,

as they jumped. But for us it was: 'One potato, two potatoes, three ...'

George Street primary school served a socially mixed, though all-white, British-born population. It closely mimicked the social composition of the road where my parents and I lived, round the corner from the school. At the top of the hill lived a bank manager and his family (my mother always maintained that all bank employees, not just managers, were paid a handsome wage so that they would not be tempted to put their hands in the till), a doctor, a couple of solicitors, a vet and a local entrepreneur who made a comfortable living out of growing watercress, if judged by the car he drove and the holidays the family took. Our house, 33 Adeyfield Road (modified by my father, who was a local authority sanitary inspector with aspirations to train as an architect), was about halfway down the hill. Next door to us lived a shop manager and next door again was the owner of a sports shop which sold mainly golf clubs and tennis racquets. On the other side were fields.

Rows of red standard roses flanked the crazy-paving path to our front door, which sported a porthole window depicting a galleon in full sail in green and amber stained glass. The low brick wall separating the garden from the road was castellated, but its heavy chains had been requisitioned for war service and were never demobbed. This loss aggrieved my mother when she heard rumours that such chains had not been used to aid the war effort at all, but rather dumped in the North Sea since no one was sure what to do with them. The rest of the garden was enclosed by a rather scrubby hedge of laurel, which gave the house its name. The leaves were a source of some interest to me, since if I scratched my name on the reverse side of a leaf and shoved it up my jumper sleeve, the warmth would cause the writing to be clearly inscribed on the other side.

The bottom of the hill was distinctly working-class – 'common', or 'rough', as my mother called it. There was a field that was used for the twice-annual fair and circus, and where children played (I was forbidden to). There was a corner shop from which you could buy penny ice lollies, or in my case I was sent to buy a 'family-sized' brick of Wall's Neapolitan ice cream – innocent of a single non-synthetic ingredient – wrapped in newspaper for 'dessert' on Sunday.

The children from the 'nether regions' included eight from an Irish family, the oldest of whom, Maureen, had plaits so long she could sit on them. Then there was Raymond, a pale, thin ('weedy') boy who always wore plimsolls and pink National Health spectacles mended with Elastoplast and whose nose continually ran. There was spiteful, mean-faced Yvonne, who used to torment me by recruiting her friends to bar my way home, and Clive, a red-headed adenoidal butcher's son and something of a ten-year-old Lothario, keen to chase girls into the bushes for a bit of a fumble. These were my classmates: Susan, the watercress grower's daughter; Sandra, whose father went up to 'town' on the train from Boxmoor station every morning with a briefcase, presumably to work in an office; Jennifer, whose father worked at the Dickinson paper mills – a substantial local employer in nearby Apsley, manufacturer of Basildon Bond writing paper (azure was the colour of choice in our house); Carol, whose father was a fireman and who lived above the shop, as it were; Michelle, a dentist's daughter; and Patsy, whose mother worked in a smart dress shop in Watford and who wore gilt earrings, heady perfume and dark red nail-varnish. 'Fast', my mother – who made do with a puff of Coty powder, a splash of 4711 cologne and a dash of Miners coral lipstick – pronounced, though I thought her the height of glamorous sophistication and envied freckled Patsy.

The grown-ups at George Street school who made the greatest impression on me were the headmistress, stern Miss Parkin, with her iron-grey hair in tight curls clinging to her skull, and the voluptuously lovely and kind teacher, Miss East, who had blonde hair and pink cheeks and who praised me excessively when, aged five, I demonstrated that I could spell yellow – a skill that has never left me.

The classrooms were hardly hives of creativity. The notion that the pictures children painted themselves should adorn the

walls had not been considered, so we spent our days gazing at
Ministry of Education-issue colour prints of farmyards, a seaside
harbour, a train station or an airport. We chanted what we could
identify – tractor, pigsty, suitcase, trawler – and then wrote the
words down with laborious pot-hooks using a wooden-handled
pen with a nib which we dipped in ink. We did 'gym' in the
playground a couple of times a week when it wasn't raining.
The only other diversion I recall was 'nature study', when a
large wireless was carried into the classroom by the only male
teacher in the school, so we could listen to a BBC educational
broadcast. Mr Robertson sat by his teaching aid throughout the
lesson like a security guard, flexing a ruler, ready to rap a
knuckle sharply if, say, a boy was to giggle, pinch his neighbour, flick paper pellets or pull the plaits of the girl sitting at
the desk in front.

Each day we sat on hard benches attached to desks that must
have been a source of constant irritation to the teachers, since
bored pupils would open the desk lid, ostensibly in search of a
pencil, only to let it go with a clatter and a splattering of ink
spilling from the china ink pot dropped into a purpose-carved
hole in the desk lid and soon stuffed with a mash of blotting
paper and pencil sharpenings. This was generally followed by
another crash: a one-note, discordant blast until errant knuckles
were rapped and the cacophony ceased.

II Not Encouraged

Every week we would labour at our desks over 'intelligence
tests', which consisted of finding the odd one out among a series

of shapes, or pairing them, or filling in the next letter or number or symbol in a sequence. This was intended to be a class-neutral test, providing a level playing field for those who came from homes containing shelves full of books and pictures and those with few such resources. The 'IQ test' was supposed to measure innate intelligence (a now much-contested concept) and provide guidance along with other tests in arithmetic and English as part of the eleven-plus exam taken towards the end of primary school, to ascertain what sort of secondary education would be most suitable for each child.

Had this system not been introduced a year before the end of the war, then as the child of lower-middle class parents who held no particular candle for the education of girls (though paradoxically my mother frequently sighed over the lack of opportunity she'd had to train as an infant school teacher), I would no doubt have been taught at an elementary school which took children from the age of five until the then statutory leaving age of fourteen. But it had been recognised before the Second World War that this system of education was not satisfactory, and the subsequent drive to improve the standard of education was part of the state provision of a better and fairer society for all, as well as being a prerequisite if Britain was to compete in the postwar world. Various committees came up with reports and recommendations during the war. The 1944 Education Act was built on previous reports, detailing how the existing education system disadvantaged less privileged children – particularly working-class boys. It was to be the first of the social reforms that built the welfare state. The 1944 Act became known as the 'Butler Act' after R. A. Butler (later to be sighed over as 'the best prime minister we never had'), who had been president of the Board of Education since 1941.

This cornerstone piece of legislation established a progressive system of free, public (i.e. state- and local-authority funded) education – primary, secondary and further. At secondary level this meant that education was determined by the notion of 'parity of esteem': a child's abilities were to be assessed by examination at eleven, and based on these results the child would be 'allocated' to a particular type of school, a scheme intended to provide equality of opportunity rather than a uniform grading system for children who might have very different abilities and interests. More academic children would go to a grammar school; technical schools would cater for those drawn to applied science or applied art; everyone else would be allocated to a secondary modern school that concentrated on practical education – mainly commercial or domestic subjects. However, things didn't quite work out like that, though the pre-war intention that the school-leaving age should be raised from fourteen to fifteen was finally implemented in 1947, and by 1972 sixteen was the age at which compulsory education ended.

The eleven-plus became not, as intended, an efficient yet benign system of allocation, but one of often bitter competition. You either passed or failed the exam, and though there were a few transfers at thirteen to 'correct' earlier misallocations, these were indeed few. Nor were many technical schools built: by 1955 there were only 302 technical schools as compared to 3,550 secondary moderns and 1,180 grammar schools. Those that were opened often lacked the resources necessary to fulfil their mission. Few catered for girls or prepared them for appropriate apprenticeship opportunities such as in the retail trade, light engineering or hairdressing.

Research found that in the 1950s, the level playing field intended by the 1944 Act was in fact still unfairly tilted. As many as nine in every ten of the unskilled and semi-skilled working class were still deprived of a grammar school education. There was not only the academic competence needed on the part of the pupil to achieve a grammar school place; there was also the expense to the child's parents of uniform (usually to be purchased at a named shop which enjoyed a monopoly), hockey sticks, mathematical instruments, school trips – all of which amounted to a serious bar for many children to taking up the places they had won.

Secondary moderns didn't seem appropriately modern in equipping children for a fast changing capitalist world, but rather became residual schools for those who didn't pass muster to get into a grammar school. Their teaching was gendered. It was presumed that girls would find domestic science most useful in the job and marriage markets, and in any case, work would be but an interlude before marriage and babies. However, as the historian of girls' education, Carol Dyhouse, points out, there was an unanticipated beneficiary of the Act: the fact that girls' educational opportunities would in future be on a par with those of boys led to greater female aspirations and achievements, a situation that would seriously challenge local education authorities' preponderance of provision for boys at grammar schools.

Grammar school pupils could sit the exams for the General Certificate of Education (GCE), which would permit entry into the sixth form, higher education and the professions. Meanwhile, the majority of pupils who attended secondary moderns left at fifteen before taking any public exams (indeed, initially such pupils were expressly prevented from taking GCEs). As late as 1961, seventy-three per cent of children left school at sixteen without having taken a public examination. In effect, at eleven years of age a child's future trajectory was decided – largely, it has to be said, as a result of class.

All this educational upheaval, moreover, left the fee-paying independent (including public) schools out of the equation, despite concerns over whether, in the words of the historian R. H. Tawney, 'the existence of a group of schools reserved for the children of the comparatively prosperous ... is or is not, as the world is today, in the best interests of the nation. It cannot be justified by the venerable device of describing privileges as liberties.' A number of Labour MPs (though not all) shared this view. Likewise, the Workers' Educational Association (WEA) was concerned that 'the position of the Public Schools is anomalous in a modern democratic society'.

At George Street, we all sat the eleven-plus: Susan, Sandra and a few others passed on to the local co-ed grammar school, most of my classmates 'failed' and were destined for one of the local secondary mods. On the basis of my results I was offered an interview at the nearby direct grant school, Berkhamsted School for Girls, founded in 1888 by a local businessman. An enlightened advocate of education for girls, he succeeded in diverting funds for the purpose from Berkhamsted School, a much older foundation, the headmaster of which in the 1930s was the father of Graham Greene, a pupil there. Our most illustrious 'old girl' was the former Clementine Hozier who married Winston Churchill, and who, during my time as a pupil, graciously turned up to perform occasional ceremonies such as the opening of a new science block.

A direct grant independent school provided twenty-five per cent of its places free (since a grant was made by the local authority) to children who had spent at least two years in a primary school and had reached the required academic standard, while the 'residuary places' would be available for children whose parents were able to pay fees, providing the child reached the same required academic standard. Almost all were single-sex schools and slightly more were for girls. Academic standards were generally high and more pupils from direct grant schools went on to university than from either grammar or independent schools.

On the whole the ethos of direct grant schools was closer to public schools than grammar schools. Our headmistress, Miss Barbara Russell, had been deputy head of Roedean under the famed Dame Emmeline Tanner – and had imported many of the social if not always the academic standards from her former position. A trim, decisive, snobbish Scotswoman – with good legs and neat ankles, according to one pupil's father – she was particularly concerned that none of her pupils should become 'bobby-soxers' and wrote an article in the local paper in effect advocating the infantilisation and desexualisation of teenage girls by keeping them away from pop music, jiving and fashionable clothes.

Berkhamsted took boarders from the age of six. There were real bricks-and-mortar houses for them and notional houses for day girls. Homework was called prep(aration), in case the thought of being at home in the evenings upset the boarders, and there was a hierarchy between those who boarded and day girls. This divide was even greater if you were a 'scholar', as we small band were known, a distinction to a degree perpetuated by the staff. Being a scholar was not a cause for praise; rather we appeared as somewhat unwelcome charity liggers. On one occasion I asked at the end of term to buy a copy of a book we had been studying – S. T. Bindoff's *Tudor England* – since, unlike fee-paying pupils whose parents were billed for their books, scholars were loaned theirs. 'But there is no need to, you are a *scholarship* pupil!' the history mistress exclaimed in amazement. I was thus dismissed as an urchin with no use for, and no money for, books beyond the purely functional and transient.

I had harboured no particular ambition to go to any specific school, and felt I had made rather a hash (or bish) of the interview for Berkhamsted. Questioned as to what my hobbies were I replied: 'Collecting postcards.' But when I was asked what I did with them, I was nonplussed. Surely the accumulation *was* the hobby? What do philatelists *do* with the stamps they collect other than stick them in albums and swap them?

Nevertheless, aware that I clearly lacked some higher sense of purpose, I henceforth started to stick my postcards into scrapbooks with some sort of taxonomy. I pondered their exchange value. Would a view of Cliftonville seafront be a fair exchange for the donkeys on Blackpool beach? The prehistoric cave paintings of Lascaux in sepia equate with the Eiffel Tower in colour? And where would I find a community of swappers? (No internet then.) Would a postcard in a newsagent's window appear to have a subtext, drawing forth inappropriate responses? The distinguished art historian and one-time editor of *Apollo* magazine, Anna Somers Cocks, was once quoted as saying that only the unhappily married are collectors. To that category could surely be added the aimless and bored: that is, most children, a lot of the time.

I felt something akin to heart-plunging despair as I shut the door of the interview room and walked towards a window framing a horse-chestnut tree in full, effervescent bloom. A conviction that I would never see the school again weighed me down like a stone in the pit of my stomach. This was coupled with a freshly minted intense desire to do so, a certainty that I would find a wider horizon, a spiritual and intellectual home there and only there among its panelled corridors, its library with books reaching up to the ceiling, its small swimming pool. I was wrong on both counts. I was offered a place. But the frothy horse-chestnut extravagance had been a false portent. The school would be a dull disappointment to me; and much more so, I to it.

My mother was pleased at my academic success, though she feared, correctly, that it would make me a snob, and particularly a cultural and intellectual snob. The watercress grower pressed a ten-shilling note into my hand, saying he realised he would not be able to speak to me now I was so elevated – his own daughter had passed to the grammar school.

There was a particular paradox about teachers at girls' schools in the postwar years. All the teachers at Berkhamsted in the mid-1950s were women. All except one were unmarried – though a young French teacher who was observed boarding a

London-bound Green Line bus after school every Friday announced her engagement and sported a half-circle diamond ring on her left hand, much to the excitement of her romantically minded pupils. Several of the staff were undoubtedly clever women with cultivated minds, who, had they been born a couple of decades later, would have taught in higher education, joined the upper ranks of the civil service, or succeeded in law, medicine, architecture, journalism or business. But career opportunities for girls were so limited when they were making their choices that teaching at a 'good school' must have seemed the most feasible option for many – an advance at least on becoming a governess, as would have been their lot in the nineteenth century. Compounding this was the invidious problem of surplus, or as the novelist George Gissing called them, 'odd' women – that is, those denied the opportunity of marriage by a variety of factors. Since the end of the nineteenth century, more baby girls had been born and/or survived than baby boys; colonial service, which sent many of the most eligible young men to the far corners of the empire, and the slaughter of the Great War had depleted the opportunities for marriage even further. And many of these women clearly resented it. They found their pupils unresponsive, giggling, unfocused – which many of us undoubtedly were.

Our nascent sexuality was also disturbing to the staff. It spoke of disobedience, uncontrollability, out-of-reachness. We wore bottle-green serge gymslips, or, when older, navy serge skirts, and blouses and green-and-pink striped ties in winter, and green-and-white gingham shirtwaister dresses in summer, with gabardine macs in winter. In summer we donned bottle-green blazers with the school motto '*Festina Lente*' – 'Hasten slowly', or more colloquially 'More haste less speed', an adage (and an oxymoron) adopted from the Greek by the Roman Emperor, Augustus – emblazoned on the breast pocket.

Over our indoor clothes we were obliged to wear the strangest garment, a pinafore that looked like a maternity smock. When new, these were indigo blue and reached to the knee, but as denim does, they soon faded, and became more of a below the bust crop-top as their wearer grew. Such vintage items were much prized and decorated with biro graffiti, their owners ignoring requests to get a replacement for as long as possible; but as pubescent breasts swelled, the pinafores began to look even odder, like shelves waiting to be filled.

Naturally, as they grew older, some girls customised their uniforms, trying to inject a little style, even sexiness, into their drab, shapeless attire: ankle socks were rolled up to make them mid-calf (though not much could be done with heavy lisle stockings); winter velour and summer panama hats were pinched into more alluring shapes than the pudding basin original, dresses pulled tight with unauthorised belts or hitched into the waist elastic of (bottle-green) knickers to make them shorter; blazer collars turned up. All this was frowned on and punished with an order mark – as was poor deportment, or hair that touched the collar, an aberration that perplexingly frequently threw one of our English mistresses into a white-knuckled fury.

Some of the teachers were engaging. The woman who taught us Latin was a riot, enacting lines from Pliny by lying on the floor for dead, or leaping on desks to brandish a sword (in fact a ruler), mock-swooning over the lyrical poetry of Catullus. I liked history since it was taught with energy and was a far-ranging narrative that included intriguing characters – predominantly men such as Richard Coeur de Lion, William Gladstone, Wat Tyler, Aethelred the Unready, Elizabeth I and Joanna the Mad – among its cast of thousands. Geography in those days was physical rather than human, and we spent many lessons drawing round plastic outlines of Britain, Europe, India, Africa or Australia and filling in the oceans, the mountain ranges and the deserts, the rivers, mineral deposits and crops. My soul, and that of many others surely, was deadened by the teaching of music 'appreciation' by a moustache-bristling woman who tried to teach us sight-reading and read out abbreviated biographies of famous composers, while her toothy blonde companion (in life as well as in the classroom, we surmised) trilled away at the piano. Musical enterprise was not encouraged. When the vicar father of a classmate, who was a talented pianist, requested that his daughter be taught the organ, his plea was turned down on the grounds that her class work was not up to standard.

Discipline was harsh and unforgiving. Order marks were doled out by teachers or prefects ('prees') for talking when waiting in line for lunch, or for taking too long to change from outdoor shoes into indoor ones, for uniform transgressions, walking on the grass, losing an exercise book. The prees stood on staircases looking down and shouting harshly. There was a lot of shouting and I often wonder how those bully girls treated their own families later. Kindness and encouragement were not the order of the day. A metaphorical bucket of cold water always seemed at hand to crush spirits that might have soared. Girls

were called buffoons, even morons, by staff, and we girls liber-
ally used words like 'retards' or 'spastics' about each other and
sneered at what would now be called an Essex accent. 'You can't
be a speech therapist,' a fellow scholar was told, 'you don't speak
properly yourself.'

Discipline marks were for really bad behaviour: transgressions such as losing your lacrosse stick. We played lacrosse so
we could have matches against smart schools like Wycombe
Abbey, Cheltenham Ladies' College or Sherborne, whereas the
two local grammar schools played hockey. I was extremely bad
at sport, and my memory of games was of being called 'rabbit'
a lot, and only ever serving as a 'ball boy' in interhouse tennis
matches. I quite liked lacrosse though, as, reputed to emanate
from the North American prairies, the game had no boundaries
and one could run cradling the ball in its leather net on a stick
into the distance, far away from the crowd of keen types in their
green Aertex shirts and serge divided skirts, feigning deaf to the
games mistress's insistent whistle.

Discipline marks were frequently doled out for answering
back, or 'insolence', for questioning a punishment, or being late
for assembly or wearing nail varnish or sneaking out of school
or the boarding house to go into town. You had to report to
your head of house to receive a punishment for a 'dissie', and on
one occasion I was set to polish the brass furniture on the door
of the prefects' common room on the logic that doing this
kneeling *en plein air* would humiliate me as fellow pupils
wandered by. It didn't really.

With little to focus my burgeoning sexual desire on, I tended
to have the odd 'crush' (or 'pash') on a prefect or teacher, and

indeed had what my friends called a 'fan club' myself – four girls, three called Jane, who followed me around at break times and after lunch. We rarely spoke.

As far as I know, the only girls who were expelled during my time were two pupils who climbed out of the dormitory window and made a buccaneer-like raid on the roof of one of the boys' school houses, hoisting up a pillow case bearing an obscene word, and a couple of boarders who had reputedly been found in bed together in their dorm. For several days after the gossip broke, I was urged by the class sophisticate to stick my hand up in an English lesson to ask what a lesbian was, which she reckoned would be good sport for all, but since I wasn't that daft I looked up the word in *The Oxford English Dictionary* instead.

Later it became de rigueur to select a boy from the boys' school to fantasise about. I chose Eddie Kempling, who impressed me as he clattered up the stairs to the top deck of the bus in his OTC (Officers' Training Corps) hobnailed boots and thick khaki uniform, his freckled face flushed with eager anticipation as he contemplated a day of combat on the playing fields – if not of Eton then at least of Berkhamsted. Again, we never spoke.

As we grew older, there were social evenings arranged largely for the boarders, but day girls were encouraged to go along too, and we stomped around the hall in mufti, circular felt skirts, or oatmeal-coloured pinafore dresses and turquoise or lime-green cotton polo necks, full tweed skirts topped by lemon Orlon cardigans, or tartan dresses with Peter Pan collars, to the music of Paul Anka's 'Diana' ('I'm so young and you're so old,/ This, my darling, I've been told') or Laurie London's 'He's Got the

Whole World in His Hands', or the haunting melodies of Buddy Holly's 'Peggy Sue' and 'That'll Be the Day', but we stopped and sat down when someone put on the record of Cole Porter's 'Miss Otis Regrets (She's Unable to Lunch Today)'.

Once a term (or was it year?) older pupils from the boys' and girls' schools met for a dance in the school hall. We girls had to submit the dresses we intended to wear for inspection a couple of weeks before the dance took place. On the evening of the dance, we sedately (or clumsily) negotiated the floor in waltzes and foxtrots, and sometimes the polka (I had only ever learned the male steps since there were no boys in school dance classes). We were scrutinised from behind the wooden pillars by members of staff to make sure that we did not dance with the same boy more than once. If we did, a heavy hand would be laid on our shoulder and we would be humiliatingly levered apart.

I did not do well at Berkhamsted School for Girls. Though I had arrived on a wave of high expectations and was put in the top division for all subjects, I soon slid down, in maths for example, to the ignominy of division three. I don't know why this decline happened. It was not an interest in boys, or pop stars or film stars, that distracted me. I read a lot – mainly 'the Russians', Chekhov, Gogol, *War and Peace*, *Crime and Punishment*. I penned short stories in what I imagined was the style of Dostoyevsky and composed what I hoped was poetry, though all I had published was an article in the school magazine, *The Berkhamstedian*, on campanology. (I had taken up bell-ringing practice on a Thursday evening at the local church, though I was terrified most of the time, as the rope whipped out of my hands as we pealed 'Bob Minor', lashing my legs and leaving painful red weals.)

In the evenings at home I listened on the Bakelite wireless in the 'lounge' to *Lost in Space*, *Paul Temple*, *The Archers*, *Mrs Dale's Diary*, music from the Albert Hall, Wigmore Hall – and of course Radio Luxemburg. Nevertheless, my academic status was inexorably lost for several years. I didn't understand why and I minded very much.

I had left behind a world of Shirleys, Wendys, Joans, Dianes, Sandras, Cheryls, Patricias and Paulines when I went to Berkhamsted, and moved into one of Carolines, Pippas, Susannahs, Oriels, Priscillas, Hermiones, Annabels, Dinahs and Joannas – even a Zenobia and a Minerva (Smith), many of whom were boarders. Several had parents abroad working in the fast-diminishing Empire, others' parents worked full time; one girl's parents lived in a Marylebone flat which was 'unsuitable for children' (why did they buy it?); a couple of girls in my class had widowed mothers who had had to take residential jobs to support their families. Saddest of all (if you consider the idea of sending young children away to school sad) were girls whose parents lived less than a mile from the school, one of whose house we walked past twice a week on the way to the school playing field for lacrosse, sometimes glimpsing her mother and little sister in the garden.

III A Glimpse Beyond

The divide was wide but I found a soulmate in Janet Hamilton, another eleven-plus 'success', who when I first met her lived across the field from our house in a development on the edge of Hemel Hempstead new town, where her father worked in the architects' department of the Development Corporation. She caught the double-decker 301C, as I did, to and from school every day, but came from a very different background. Her parents were professionals, recently returned from Australia. Her father, Humphrey, later became a government planning inspector; her mother, Mollie, the daughter of one of Scotland's first female graduates, was a part-time teacher who hosted coffee mornings. At my house we had elevenses – Camp coffee and a Rich Tea biscuit or a custard cream – but no one was ever invited.

The Hamiltons had interesting friends: one a chiropodist, another a GP who played the piano to near-professional stand-ard, several immigrants from Nazi Germany and Austria. The group were supporters of progressive education and patrons of Steiner and Montessori schools; they listened to classical or folk music on their radiograms and subscribed to the efficacy of herbal remedies and left-wing politics; they were regular stal-warts of CND, joining if not the first then certainly the second of the Aldermaston protest marches. Janet's brother went to a prep school and later was a fee-paying pupil at the local boys' school. Had Janet not won a scholarship from her progressive plate-glass primary school, would she, a girl, have had her fees paid so she could attend the girls' school, or would she have taken up a place at the local grammar school, I wonder? When the family moved from their Hemel Hempstead Development Corporation house to the outskirts of Berkhamsted, their new home was modern, with plate-glass windows, David Whitehead fabric curtains, spindly chairs, cacti on the windowsills and a rabbit in a hutch in the back garden. I loved going there: the family was so welcoming and I knew that this was how I would like to live. When my school report complained that I had little respect for authority, Mollie Hamilton chuckled and said that was no bad thing: look at Winston Churchill.

Janet and I had our own language, a mixture of what we fondly imagined was Shakespearean English and a sort of back-chat, which we kept up much longer than we should have. In a town where there was nothing much to do, she joined the local branch of the Cactus & Succulent Society of Great Britain, and I went along for the company. I also spent an inordinate amount of time in church, bell-ringing, or doing other church-related activities, excusing myself to Janet by saying that the choirboys were very dishy – which they certainly were not. But what else was there to do after *Two-Way Family Favourites* and *Educating Archie* were over on a Sunday?

I went to Sunday school from a young age, taken by a kind local grande dame, Mrs Hart, and spent many hours carefully colouring in pictures of Jesus as a baby in a manger or as a man triumphantly entering Jerusalem surrounded by the crowds waving palm leaves. I don't think we got much further in Christ's chronology than that: it might have been considered a bit sensationalist to colour in Jesus on the Cross, red blood dripping from his stigmata.

When I was a little older, I went to Bible-reading classes in the home of one of the young curates, where he played us sacred music on his wind-up gramophone and we discussed why sex before marriage was a sin. At about this time, I was confirmed by the Bishop of St Albans. At one of the final classes held by the vicar in preparation for our confirmation, we were asked whether we thought we were ready to take this step. This brought my anxieties to a head. We had never discussed theology or divinity or faith either in church or at school. All I knew about Christianity, apart from Bible stories, was a sketchy narrative of its history. I had been on a pilgrimage to St Albans Cathedral at Easter, where I'd become acquainted with the exemplary stories of the noble martyrs who died for their faith, admired the tomb of the eponymous St Alban and then had a hearty breakfast prepared by the good women parishioners in the abbey hall.

But did I believe in God? What did that mean? What was faith? Where, or rather how, did it fit in with scientific explanations of the beginning of creation? How would I know if I had faith? How would I behave if I did? Or, conversely, if I didn't?

I treated going to church as something you did on a Sunday, much like going to the church youth club on a Tuesday evening and shopping at the local market on a Saturday morning. Sometimes I was deeply moved by the ceremonies of religious practice the hymns, the psalms, the organ music, the church overflowing with black- or scarlet-robed solemn men of God when our curate was ordained. After I had been confirmed (my doubts never expressed) I found taking communion – the deep rich Marmitey taste of the wine, the delicate dissolve of the wafer on the tongue, 'the body and blood of Christ which is given for you ...' – a deeply sensual experience. Perhaps if I'd had the opportunity to read Bishop John Robinson's hugely controversial book *Honest to God* at that time, it would have resolved some of my anxieties, since Robinson explored the tricky idea of belief in God in a secular age. This was not so much God above us, but God amongst us. But it wasn't published until 1963, and by that time my focus had shifted.

Whatever I might have thought of Christianity's doctrinal aspects, I was not so sure about its lived manifestations. Once when a curate's wife was taken into hospital, the women in the congregation pitched in to help with the domestic chores, and as payback were able to gossip far and wide about how grey her children's vests and the bed linen were, how the oven didn't look as if it had been cleaned for years.

The vicar at our parish church of St Mary's was an urbane, handsome man with a snub-nosed wife – and four adorable snub-nosed children whose heads he used to pause to pat as he made his slow and stately way to the altar, the crucifix on a chain around his waist jangling slightly. But then it emerged that he had been keeping company with an elegant gimlet-eyed parishioner; they would go off riding far into the hills together, she in a fetching hacking jacket and riding hat with an eye-level net veil, until one of the parishioners refused to lend the reverend and his lady her horses any longer, so the hanky-panky, if that is what it was, stopped – or maybe relocated.

Janet and I, and our school friends Ann and Penny, were occasionally allowed to take the Green Line bus which connected us to the metropolis. Green Line buses figured large in my life in the outer London suburbs, as they did for the historian Tony Judt, bestowing what felt like the first stamp in a non-existent passport to a wider world. We would usually go to the Natural

History Museum or, at Mollie's suggestion, to an exhibition at the V&A, or the Royal Academy. And we shopped in C&A Modes, buying a houndstooth-check pencil skirt each for 19s. 11d., and trying on dresses in one of the many little 'Madam' shops that existed then in Oxford Street, where the sales assistants were largely paid on commission and so were obliged to push their wares to a sometimes off-putting extent.

Janet was good at art, though this was not regarded as an important subject in the school curriculum, and she went on eventually to train and practise as a landscape architect. My bent lay in debating – endlessly arguing in competitions at school, in youth clubs and junior road safety forums for, say, the end of the death penalty, of school uniform, of apartheid, of compulsory religious education, and for more zebra crossings and the lowering of the voting age. In a school that pronounced itself apolitical (which meant in effect unquestioningly on the side of the status quo), Janet and I were the only members of the rather ineffectual Labour Club, which I think we started. ('You can't vote *Labour*,' a fellow pupil exploded. 'Only *miners* vote Labour.') But long before we could vote, Janet and I joined her mother in pushing leaflets through letterboxes to counteract the posters that were being pasted up all over town in 1959: 'Save us from Floud', the Labour candidate for the Hemel Hempstead constituency. We were unsuccessful. Bernard Floud was soundly beaten by the Conservative, James Allason, who polled a majority of 8,365 votes. Allason was the successor to Viscountess Frances Davidson, who had taken over her husband's seat when he was elevated to the peerage in 1937 and retired from the Commons at the 1959 election. In the early days of women MPs most – including Irene Adams, Margaret Wintringham, Agnes Hardie, the sister-in-law of Keir Hardie, and later Lena Jeger and Ann Cryer – were either there as a result of 'widow's succession', or like Viscountess Astor and Lady Davidson had succeeded to their husbands' seats when they went to the Lords. However, all proved to be admirable MPs, regardless of their nepotistic route to a seat in the Commons.

By the time I reached the fifth form, GCE time, I was called to the headmistress's study, as were my fellow pupils one by one, for 'careers advice'. 'I understand you have considerable literary ability,' she said (presumably thinking of the very appreciative report of a composition I had written on 'colour', which in fact was largely a mash-up of a Revlon advertisement for a 'sun-kissed, peach' lipstick; a short extract from Oscar Wilde's 'The Ballad of Reading Gaol' – 'that little patch of blue which prisoners call the sky' – and another from the Song of Solomon). 'I suggest a career in librarianship.' I slunk away.

In 1960 there was still the presumption that even if a girl went to university or teacher-training college, her ultimate ambition was to marry a successful man, have a family and develop cultivated pursuits or philanthropic voluntary work as her mother probably had. This was three years before the Robbins Report that confirmed the expansion of the higher education sector, when new 'plate-glass' universities such as Sussex, Essex, York, Lancaster, the University of East Anglia and Heriot-Watt in Edinburgh offered places for more students – male or female – to study a broader range of subjects if they so chose. In the meantime, I was not regarded as university material, though admittedly only six girls in my year were: among them Lydia, the daughter of the Director of Education for Hertfordshire, went to the Royal Free Hospital Medical School; Ann, who had a rather enviable family background in fairground operations and was pony-mad, won a place to read philosophy and English at Nottingham. The privileged six were alone within a cohort of some thirty girls, though others would go on to achieve successful careers in professions such as nursing, social work and teaching.

Out of the 22,426 students who took first degrees in 1960, 16,851 were men and just 5,575 were women. When it came to MAs, MScs, PhDs or similar, only 279 women managed that hurdle, compared to 2,994 men. This was a failure of ambition rather than a lack of talent; a failure that pervaded so many schools and families. There is a striking number of my contemporaries who left school with no path into higher education or further training mapped out for them, yet who subsequently with no help or guidance from the school found their own way to university, art school or other gateways to the professions.

At home there was no encouragement to think about university. My mother was clear that marriage was my destiny, reminding me that everyone knew that men didn't like clever women. When I expressed an interest in reading law, her scorn knew no bounds. 'I suppose you see yourself as Hancock, Hancock & Wells,' she mocked, instancing the brass plate outside the local solicitors in the high street as an example of unimaginable and inappropriate ambition. Interviews were arranged for me at various secretarial colleges. I declined to attend. I might not know what I wanted to do, but it certainly wasn't that – though as a writer now who still laboriously types with one finger I wish I had learned touch-typing skills, while bypassing shorthand and avoiding learning how to keep your boss's diary up to date and his dry-cleaning collected.

Unlike Sylvia Plath, sitting in the metaphorical crotch of a fig tree, no tempting figs representing the choice between a glittering career or a brilliant marriage glistened just out of reach for me. All I knew was that I wanted out.

Chapter Four

Old Town Blues

Most summer evenings, after a tea comprising slices of rather stale white bread spread thinly with butter and jam or Heinz sandwich spread, a slice of sponge cake, and on Sundays tinned peaches or a Chivers jelly served from a cut-glass bowl, I would take a book, or probably more often a comic, to sit in the field next to our house. It might have been *School Friend*, or more likely *Girl*. This was the sister publication in the Reverends Chad Varah/Marcus Morris stable to *Eagle* for boys and the older sibling to *Swift* and *Robin* for younger children – though it was not clear why the bird nomenclature wasn't sustained and *Girl* called 'Starling' or, more predictably, 'House Martin'. Like most of my friends, I lapped up the adventures of the tomboyish school friends Wendy and Jinx, the fragile-looking Belle of the Ballet, the cartoon figure of the naïve Lettice Leefe ('the Greenest Girl in the School' – where green meant naïve rather than environmentally minded), and read of career opportunities to 'cook in the sky' (become an air hostess) or work as a hospital almoner.

I would sit for hours in the long grass by the side of an overgrown, defunct railway branch line – axed long before Beeching wielded his in the mid-1960s, closing more than 2,000 stations and 4,000 miles of rail lines in an attempt to stop the haemorrhage of money from the railways.

Sometimes I would take a copy of Arthur Mee's *Children's Newspaper*. Or very occasionally a borrowed copy of the *Young Elizabethan*, a glossy magazine, priced at an unaffordable (to me) 2s. 6d. a month. Aimed at grammar school children, it contained articles on literature, art and music. The magazine had been called *Collins Magazine for Boys and Girls* until two weeks before the coronation of Elizabeth II on 2 June 1953. The change of name was to honour the new queen, and also to underline the fresh energy it was hoped that this young female monarch would bring to a postwar-weary Britain, still in the only gradually loosening grip of austerity. As an adjective 'Elizabethan' had considerable traction in the early years of her reign, but it never came to define the period as Georges I, II and III, Victoria or Edward VII had. The subsequent century would be counted in and out by decades.

One of the *Young Elizabethan*'s editors was Kaye Webb, whose husband Ronald Searle illustrated many of the issues, and would later become famous for his St Trinian's books about an invented gothic girls' boarding school with anarchic, messy pupils. Webb went on to run the children's list at Penguin, Allen Lane's paperback phenomenon of the 1930s. The Puffin imprint included books by Roald Dahl, C. S. Lewis, Rosemary Sutcliff and Clive King, whose *Stig of the Dump* I would read to my children over and over again (at their request) in the 1970s.

My own childhood reading had been rather less imaginative, with the possible exception of Arthur Ransome. The books that were read to me, or later I read myself, included Enid Blyton's *Malory Towers* and her Famous Five adventures, the series of *Flower Fairies* books, and Milly-Molly-Mandy and her tiresome 'little friend Susan', by Joyce Lankester Brisley. My favourite reading as a child was a series of books by the Welsh writer Gwynedd Rae about Mary Plain, a small orphaned bear who lives with her relatives in the bear pits of Berne Zoo, though she is anthropomorphic and can talk. Mary is befriended by two visitors, the Fur-Coat Lady and the Owl Man, so named because he wears horn-rimmed spectacles. Another absolute favourite was *The Family from One End Street*, written and illustrated by Eve Garnett, first published in 1937, about Mr and Mrs Ruggles, he a dustman, she a washerwoman, and their numerous children. It was an unusual book since it portrayed a happily chaotic working-class family, whereas most children's books at the time were about the middle classes having fun at boarding school, playing japes and riding their ponies.

However, such books were long behind me as I made my way to read in the field in the early 1950s. Lying in the grass, sucking the sweetness out of dusty clover flowers as I turned the pages, I occasionally glanced up at the skyline where banks of new houses appeared to be advancing down the hill, stopping like an avalanche just short of our pebble-dashed house. It looked as if the rows of new homes were aiming to join up with the old town of Hemel Hempstead, nestling in the valley below.

I No New Jerusalem

The question of housing dominated political debate in the post-war years and preoccupied the minds of many of the electorate. By the end of the Second World War, up to one million houses in Britain had been destroyed or damaged beyond repair, leaving many thousands of families homeless. Some moved into the already overcrowded houses of parents or relatives, living in a back bedroom, getting on each other's nerves in spaces hardly large enough for one family, let alone two.

The new homes I watched being built were a concrete (actually bricks and mortar) manifestation of the political and social concerns of the postwar years. Housing would continue to dominate debate and form the key plank of both the Conservative and Labour election manifestos until the 1960s. But this time there was no grandiose talk of 'Homes for Heroes' as there had been after the First World War. In 1945 Labour had prophesied that:

> Housing will be one of the greatest and one of the earliest tests of a Government's real determination to put the nation first. Labour's pledge is firm and direct – it will proceed with a housing programme with the maximum practical speed until every family in this island has a good standard of accommodation. That may well mean centralising and pooling building materials and components by the State, together with price control. If that is necessary to get the houses as it was necessary to get the guns and planes, Labour is ready. And housing ought to be dealt with in relation to good town planning – pleasant

surroundings, attractive lay-out, efficient utility services, including the necessary transport facilities.

However, despite indications of nationalisation and the control and direction of resources, as had been the wartime pattern, 'Jerusalem' (the William Blake poem Labour Party members sang alongside 'The Red Flag' at the closing of its party conferences) was not built then, or indeed ever, in England's green and pleasant land. Frustrated by the lack of homes, some people became militant, staging protests and rent strikes, squatting in houses requisitioned during the war and subsequently vacated, occupying army barracks and military encampments. Since squatting was a civil not a criminal offence, and public opinion was in general sympathetic to the plight of the squatters, the authorities proved fairly complicit about the occupations. Until, that is, the movement became not only about finding homes but more politically motivated: an indictment of the government's inability to fulfil its pledge. Squatters, organised in some cases by activists from the Communist Party of Great Britain, started to occupy empty flats in London's West End, invoking threats of prosecution for trespass, while others supported rent strikes in East End tenements that had been a disgrace even before the war.

Some homeless families were moved into hastily patched-up war-damaged properties, but the government's immediate solution was to build temporary housing, an initiative that had been started during the war for those bombed out of their homes. However, when the 1947 programme of erecting prefabricated houses on site ended in 1951, only 15,623 prefabs had been built as their cost had proved to be greater than the cost of conventional housing, and much of the material needed for construction had gone for export in the drive to pay off Britain's humongous war debts. Though the prefabs were small, they had an indoor bathroom, a modern kitchen and a small patch of garden, and delighted most of the families who were allocated one. They were intended as a short-term solution – ten years at the most – though in practice most lasted much longer than that and some are still lived in today.

An alternative for those made homeless as a result of the war was the chance of a fresh start outside the big cities in one of the satellite new towns, originally conceived of in Abercrombie's Greater London Plan of 1944, drawn up to get former slum dwellers out of the fetid and devastated urban slums. These were part of what historians have come to call the 'postwar settlement', along with the founding of the National Health Service,* greater educational opportunities, baby clinics and funded playgroups, all designed to give the postwar generation a new start, an improved chance in life after the most terrible war in history.

My home town of Hemel Hempstead, some twenty-five miles from London and beyond what became known as the 'Green Belt' encircling the metropolis, had been designated in 1946 as the third of the Labour government's new towns after Stevenage and Crawley. Lying on the grass in the summer of 1951 by that defunct railway line, I watched the new town encroaching week by week, month by month.

* Women were probably the greatest beneficiaries of the NHS since, not covered by their husbands' national insurance contributions, many lived for years with chronic conditions such as prolapse of the womb, varicose veins and fibroids, sometimes with inadequate pre- and post-natal care.

The parvenu bore every mark of the time and expectations of its naissance and completion. The centre of the new town was called Queen's Square; there was a flagpole outside the town hall with the 1951 insignia of the Festival of Britain atop it; thoroughfares were designated Everest Way, Hillary Avenue, Tenzing Road, in honour of the successful ascent of Everest in 1953, news of which was announced on the day of the queen's coronation. This triumph was taken to mean that even if Britain was fast losing an empire, she was still able to conquer its highest peaks.

These new towns might have seemed like a blueprint for a better Britain to the planners and politicians, but to existing residents of Hemel Hempstead the new town seemed an unwanted intrusion. This was despite the fact that it was designed by the distinguished architect, Geoffrey Jellicoe, who imaginatively included water gardens and generous squares in his plans. The architect and social scientist Judith Ledeboer, who had been praised before the war in the architectural press for wielding 'more influence – and getting more work done than any six pompous and prating males', was also involved.

For most of my parents' neighbours, there was little rejoicing that the country seemed at last to be beginning to get to grips with its housing problems. They were too unhappy that Hemel Hempstead, established as a settlement in the eighth century and boasting one of the finest Norman churches in the country, could no longer be seen as a predominantly middle-class market town.

I was less critical. Since my school friend Janet's father was an architect employed by the Development Corporation, the family lived for a while in one of the houses I had watched being built, and I admired the clean functional layout and light rooms, the novelty of built-in cupboards and Formica worktops in the uncluttered kitchen. And, not being particularly fond of the old town, I was indifferent to the change. I felt little affection for the pharmacy where the chemist's wife dressed in imitation of (or perhaps homage to) Queen Mary, in pastel chiffon dresses, with a different-coloured toque to match every outfit, several rows of pearls, and sported a parasol which she tapped impatiently on the ground if she had to wait in a shop queue like everyone else. Nor for Keen's the butcher, where animal carcasses hung in the shop window, blood mingled with sawdust on the floor, and the blood won out in the olfactory contest. No affection either for the haberdasher that still had wires strung high up with brass capsules that carried payment from the assistant to the cash office, and brought change and a receipt back the same way. Nor indeed for the owner, Myrtle herself, who made a great production of wrapping a packet of sanitary towels in a lumpy brown paper parcel so, she avowed, no one could guess what was inside.

My parents, however, shared the general distress. My father opined that the new town houses were 'damned ugly' and looked 'jerry-built' to him, and that we could no longer claim to live 'in the country' (could we ever?). My mother was mortified to realise that she was now caught in an advancing pincer movement: common at the bottom of the road, now common at the top too. What hope for her scramble into the difficult-to-penetrate middle classes with their oblique differentials?

II Respectable and Solitary

What did my mother mean by 'common'? It was a word of
disdain on her lips with no connotations of normality or ordin-
ariness. Ironically, and I am sure unbeknown to her, 'common'
was itself regarded as common parlance by the better educated.
For her 'common' was a distancing word laced with criticism of
all the external signs of not trying hard enough to play by the
unspoken rules and obey the conventions of 'civilised' life to
which she aspired. In her view, women signified their commonness by having peroxide-blonde hair, smoking in the street, or
wearing slippers, aprons and metal curlers while out shopping.
Both sexes when common ate in the street (especially bags of
chips), and the men donned boiler suits to dismantle their
motorbikes at the kerbside with a bottle of beer at their elbow.
In essence these people, and the mothers who cuffed their children on the pavement, were making domestic life and strife
transparent, for all to see; turning inside foibles outside, eschewing privacy, that precious lower-middle-class achievement.

I don't think my mother regarded commonness as particularly
contagious, though I was sent to elocution lessons at Stella
Clarke's, the local ballet school. With separate schools, churches,
halls and shopping parades, there was little fusion of old and new
towns – at least that was certainly the case in Hemel Hempstead.

My parents had a profound deference born of historic
circumstances. Although my father had been too young to fight
in the First World War and borderline too old to fight in the
Second, both had handed-down memories of the workhouse,
the final indignity and institutionalisation of the indigent, the

profligate, the sick and the old. Both had lived through the Depression of the Thirties and the seemingly intractable problems of unemployment and underemployment, made profoundly humiliating by the dreaded 'Means Test' that pried unremittingly into your home, your family life, your financial circumstances, sometimes even removing objects from your home in full view of gawping neighbours to set against any benefits you might receive.

Living in the southeast of England, neither of my parents had been as directly affected by these indignities as those living in the northeast, the lowlands of Scotland, the valleys of South Wales, the clay-quarrying industrial areas of Cornwall. But this, and what he regarded as the fearful divisive anarchy of the 1926 General Strike, had instilled in my father a fear of the power of the boss class and he kept his head down at work, near-worshipping our kindly local doctor who, in pre-NHS days, was known to be generous to those he suspected could not pay for his services and was prepared to come to a sickbed in the middle of the night if summoned.

The Thirties radicalised some, turning them to communism or at least socialism. They reaffirmed my father's conservatism – and Conservatism: '*They* know how to govern. That Labour shower couldn't run a whelk stall' (or, presumably, a piss-up in a brewery). You needed someone to look up to, to defer to, to respect for reasons of class and position, to be in charge of the country.

Surely one of the saddest things about the attachment to privacy ('keeping yourself to yourself' and 'minding your own business') and the slavish respect for conventions and anxiety about the opinion of others was how few friends my parents had: hardly anyone ever came to the house. There were the actively church-going Bill and Hilda, friends from pre-marriage days who lived in Ealing (or probably Hanwell), who sometimes brought their Girl Guide-leader daughter, Mary, for tea on Sunday, when my mother would make her signature dish of cream-filled chocolate eclairs. There were Ruby and Stan, who also had an adopted daughter Carol, who was about my age. They owned a hardware shop in Stanmore, but there was a falling-out over some disputed payment for a Cornishware pottery jug, and the matter was never resolved, the breach never healed.

For what must have been at least thirty years, my parents' next-door neighbours were Mr and Mrs Cushion on one side and Mr and Mrs Glenister on the other. However, there were no neighbourly exchanges over the fence: no cups of sugar were ever borrowed, nor were first names ever used, they all remained Mr and Mrs. The only people we saw regularly were family. At Christmas we went to stay with my mother's sister and husband and three children in Gloucestershire. Very occasionally my mother's cousin Horace and his wife Edna motored down from their home in Walsall en route to a seaside holiday. And perhaps twice a year, we would drive to see a rather jolly cousin of my mother's, Kath. She lived in Pinner with her husband Jimmy, who smoked a pipe and pontificated from an armchair which I never saw him leave, and their civil service typist daughter, Patricia, whose clothes were passed on to me when I was older, though I stuffed them to the back of the wardrobe and always declined to wear them.

One Sunday a month or so we would drive to visit my father's kindly widowed sister, Rose, who lived with her brother and sister-in-law in Bushey, to watch *Sunday Night at the London Palladium* since we did not have a television. Though my father was determined that we'd never own one, I was enamoured of the tiny flickering black-and-white screen, though the only time I saw it, apart from these Sunday excursions, was when my friend Susan's grandfather could be persuaded to let us watch the marionette puppets, Mr Turnip and Muffin the Mule, on his set.

My father, Charles, was a good-looking man whose black hair he would let me style when my stifling boredom reached a pitch on a Sunday afternoon. He was by temperament solitary and stoical, perhaps as a result of a difficult childhood and the loss of his much-loved older brother in the Battle of the Somme. He was one of the millions whom the two wars had left with a deep, unspoken grief for life. Though kindly and domesticated, he was an anxious, private soul: 'decent', I think would be the epithet that best described him. He did not enjoy the camaraderie of the pub. His father had been an alcoholic and he regarded all drink as the work of the devil, and every year would stuff a ten-shilling note in the envelope the Salvation Army pushed through the letterbox. The most alcohol that was ever consumed in our house was a small glass of Harvey's Bristol Cream at Christmas.

Charles was something of an autodidact. He was one of five children of a feckless father who gambled as well as drank, and a mother I can recall only dimly as small, quiet and kindly, wearing a rusty black dress and presenting me with a single barley sugar or pear drop sweet when we visited them. There had been no money for education beyond elementary school, so my father, born in 1898, left at the statutory age of twelve. But he was not without ambition and a desire to improve his lot. He had bought the full set of Charles Dickens's novels (from a *Daily Express* special offer) and even designed a special niche in the sitting-room wall above the wireless to house them. He read them all in sequence from beginning to end, and then started reading them all over again, since he had forgotten some details he wanted to recall. It was an enterprise somewhat akin to painting the Forth Bridge, and he never read any other books to my knowledge, but he certainly had the Great Boz under his belt.

As Charles's aspirations towards a medical career were, unfortunately, unthinkable, he had applied himself to home study in order to qualify to become a sanitary inspector, poring over textbooks every evening and copying down rows of figures and chunks of text in a strange, distinctive, elaborate hand which looked almost like Arabic script. He must have worked very hard because he seems to have achieved the certification necessary to apply for a job with Hemel Hempstead Rural District Council, where he spent his working days poking around drains, checking out sewage works and visiting what were apparently appallingly insanitary homes. 'I could write a book, I've got so many stories to tell of things I've seen and homes I've been to and people I've met,' he used to say. Of course he never did, but I wish he had told me some of those stories. Meanwhile, he never gave up his ambition to be a surveyor or, even better, an architect. He continued to study and is credited with having helped to design a cricket pavilion for a nearby village.

My father had been a Boy Scout leader at one time. I have a photograph of him in khaki shirt and shorts, with his Stetson-like Scout hat and a leather toggle to keep his neckerchief in place; but something went wrong there and he resigned in a huff and we never saw his fellow Scout leader, Reg, and his wife Nancy and their two boys with whom we used to go camping, again. I hope that it was not the kind of misdemeanour that we too often unfairly associate with Scout leaders today, but I simply cannot believe it was, and such a dreadful thing was never even hinted at by anyone. After that, the only people Charles ever spoke of at home were 'Nother in the office' and his boss, Mr Lightbody, and he never saw them socially. He had no hobbies as far as I can recall, though he made me a swing in the garden when I was a child with wire encased in a cut-up rubber hose, and years later made a shelf for my new house (which unfortunately collapsed a couple of weeks after it was put up, breaking every object on it and nearly killing the cat). On winter evenings and on Sunday afternoons, my father endlessly played patience and solitaire (both rather movingly symbolic) and taught me to play gin rummy. And late Saturday afternoon would be devoted to checking the football pools. The names Preston North End, Blackburn Rovers, Plymouth Argyle still transport me back to the boxy Rexine armchair, with the brown velvet seat and the linen cushion embroidered in lazy-daisy stitch of a crinolined lady carrying a parasol, where my father sat in his grey sleeveless pullover, knitted by my mother, metic-ulously ticking off the tiny squares with a ballpoint pen.

In his mid-eighties, my father had a series of strokes and the final one landed him in hospital where, when I visited, he looked at me with pleading eyes, but was unable to articulate what he wanted. To go home, I imagine. I knew he was dying but no one could predict when. One day in February 1985 I had to go to Cambridge for work. I rang the hospital from a phone box every couple of hours, and when I rang at four o'clock in the afternoon, the ward sister said: 'I think you had better come now', so I drove at reckless speed through the gloaming, but arrived too late. My father had died twenty minutes earlier. So he died in a solitary state, in some way as he had lived. I managed to stiffen my resolve to pay my respects to his body in the hospital mortuary, but when I was handed a plastic dustbin liner, the paucity of his possessions at the end – pyjamas, slippers and toothbrush, with no books, letters, or photographs – caused me to break down in racking sobs. At his funeral a few days later the mourners consisted of me, my children and two unknown church-goers, my mother being too frail by then to attend.

My mother had the Townswomen's Guild, the Mothers' Union and the church choir every Sunday and the town choir alternate Mondays, but no circle of friends to come to tea, and there was no popping next door or down the street for a gossip. There were no coffee bars to meet in when I was a child, and tea rooms were for holidays or excursions, not to meet your friends or neighbours for a chat. My generation has made more opportunities to gather with other women in book clubs or to meet a few 'girl friends' in wine bars. My daughter's generation is even more convivial, with the dinner parties we used to have perhaps once a month giving way to more frequent informal suppers or family lunches, or coming back with friends after an evening out to play music and drink more wine, once the children are asleep. I suppose my mother could have joined a bridge club – though I doubt if she was ever invited to: so apart from beetle drives in aid of the church roof, her sorority was sadly limited.

'You don't have children in order to leave them,' she would sniff when a neighbour arranged for a local teenager to babysit her children while she accompanied her husband to a Rotary or Masonic dinner. A cinema matinee or the local am-dram society's annual production of *Brigadoon*, or Terence Rattigan's *Separate Tables* were my mother's only occasional outings away from me. And family holidays were precisely that, no matter that our family was so small.

Above all else and for years, my mother had wanted a fur coat. Finally, some of her shares in the Inveresk Paper Company came good and she bought a second-hand musquash fur coat from Swears & Wells at auction. I still have it. Every spring and autumn as I sort out my winter or summer clothes, I resolve to get rid of it. But I never can. It is a symbol to me of a sad mixture of the aspiration and loneliness that I suspect were the handmaidens of so many women in the 1950s. My mother did not live a fur-coat life. The only time she wore the coat to my knowledge was to a dinner we gave at Stone's Chop House in Panton Street for my twenty-first birthday in 1964. I wish so much she had not had to buy it for herself, and that my father (who would faithfully give her a bottle of 4711 cologne for every single birthday and Christmas) had had the money or the imagination to buy it for her.

Chapter Five

Expectations

———

In February 1961, aged seventeen, I got married in a bombed-out church in Clifton, Bristol. The city had suffered extensive damage during the Blitz in January 1941, when the weather was so bitterly cold that icicles formed by water from the firemen's hoses hung several feet long like glistening, needle sharp stalactites. The church had lost many of its roof tiles, and tarpaulins were still tied firmly round the most solid-looking remnants of the remaining stone structure, to keep it partially dry; it was very cold and not at all windproof, and what stained glass was left in the windows was cracked. My future husband, George, and I (we had bypassed the usual rite of an engagement) had chosen this somewhat unlikely venue since it had a reputation for the quality of its music (the organ miraculously had only suffered a couple of broken and easily repairable pipes) and it was 'high' – an Anglo-Catholic house of God where the pungent smell of incense was wafted around as often as possible during services. Even today, I imagine, no one at its services is expected to evangelise, grasping their fellow pew-sharers warmly by the hand and murmuring 'Jesus be with you'.

I wore a white damask wedding dress hired from Moss Bros in Covent Garden, with a veil inexpertly anchored (by me) with very visible kirby grips, keeping on a wax-flower tiara. Wedding photographs, taken at cut-price rate by the photographer from one of the newspapers in the group whose graduate training scheme the man I was marrying had joined, show me waving (at whom, I wonder?) a trailing bouquet of yellow roses and white freesias as we, the newly-weds, came out of the church. I had promised to love, honour, cherish and obey, for better, for worse, in sickness and in health ... forsaking all others until death us do part. Within two decades, I am ashamed to say, I had broken more than one of those solemn vows and my husband had almost certainly reneged on at least a couple too.

We were followed by Janet, my best friend from school, who was rather glumly (or so it looks in the photographs later stuck in a white 'Wedding Album' embossed with horseshoe and silver bells) taking the role of adult bridesmaid – hardly a matron of honour since she was also seventeen at the time. Our best man had been a friend of my husband's at Oxford University. In fact, his first choice had been another close friend, a mature fellow student at Balliol who had been a market gardener before plunging into academic study; but he had declined, saying he abhorred weddings (though he was at the time married to someone who was reputed to look like Moira Shearer in *The Red Shoes*) since he maintained that he had no idea what 'I love you' actually meant. This seemed a respectable position for someone studying PPE – philosophy, politics and economics – where the dominant turn was expounded by Freddie (A. J.) Ayer's writings on the philosophical formulation of logical positivism, though I suspect that such literalist integrity may have contributed something to the breakdown of his marriage later on.

We were married by Canon Plummer, the new vicar of my mother's parish church, St Mary's. Several of my somewhat bemused school friends attended. The reception was held at a hotel perched on the edge of Avon Gorge, in the shadow of Isambard Kingdom Brunel's magnificent suspension bridge spanning the vertiginously steep ravine. My father made a speech saying that at my christening I had looked around in bewilderment, wondering what on earth was happening; he wondered if it was the same on my wedding day. This was a somewhat loaded but in fact insightful remark. As we drove away in my new husband's red Triumph Spitfire sports car, the obligatory empty paint cans and a kettle clanking from the bumper, the assembled guests (including a number of my husband's journalist colleagues, invited by him to drop in when they had finished their shift, somewhat to the alarm of my father, who was footing the bill for the reception) waved us off, and one called, 'Goodbye Mr Gardiner, goodbye Mrs Gardiner.' I was dumbstruck. It sounded like an entirely different identity, one I was wary of assuming, an adulthood I was not sure that I wanted to embrace despite the fact that I had been desperate to leave childhood. At that moment it felt there had been no transition, no plateau on which to reflect and draw breath.

Since we had failed to raise the wherewithal to go to Paris, we honeymooned in Lyme Regis, walking along the Cobb by the side of the toffee-coloured, troubled-looking sea, scrambling up cliff paths in the sleeting February rain until we were driven by the cold and wet into cafés for tea or to idle away a couple of hours in the local museum of Mary Anning's fossils. Changing for dinner in the hotel we couldn't really afford, after a glass of fino sherry, I remember we chose *veau marengo* and *boeuf stroganoff* followed by *crème caramel*, from a leather-covered menu that made no concessions to seasonality.

I An Impasse Resolved

Seventeen was an inauspiciously young age at which to marry – the average age for women marrying in the early 1960s was around twenty-two or twenty-three. Why was there this rush to the altar? I was not about to become that figure of moral panic, 'a gymslip mother'. Was it a long carry-over from the war, when there were both emotional and pragmatic reasons for haste? Your fiancé or boyfriend might be killed and you wanted your future sorted, your status acknowledged, a clarity of vision when peace came. In addition, a married allowance would be paid to the wives of those serving in the forces, a wife would be eligible for a widow's pension and a married woman could join the queue for local authority housing for her family. This wartime perception was carried throughout the Fifties by the retention of National Service until 1960, with young men deployed to fight in the Korean War from 1950.

Perhaps it was a continuation of the early-century fear of surplus women (though by 1945 that was no longer the case and indeed a shortfall of women was predicted – 'Girls are getting scarce and the outlook for men is alarming,' warned the

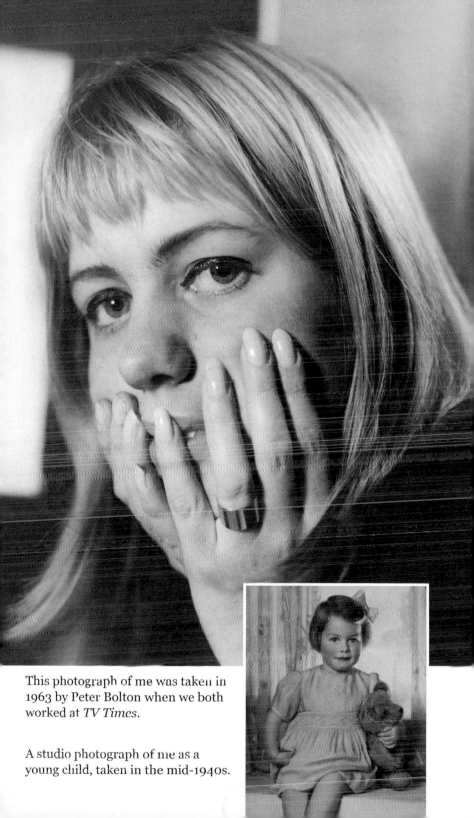

This photograph of me was taken in 1963 by Peter Bolton when we both worked at *TV Times*.

A studio photograph of me as a young child, taken in the mid-1940s.

Bomb damage in Balham, London, during the Second World War.

Children at a VE Day street party in Wimbledon, London, 1945.

Woman pushing a pram in front of council houses in Hemel Hempstead, a new town in Hertfordshire, 1954.

My mother and me on holiday in Swanage, Dorset, in 1952.

At Berkhamsted School for Girls with my friend Janet (right), late 1950s.

Me in 1954 as Gillian Wells, at school in a contemplative mood.

Cover of *Picture Post* magazine, 1952. The magazine was liberal and anti-fascist – it ceased publication in 1957.

Debutantes and their mothers queuing outside Buckingham Palace, 1957.

My wedding on 18th February 1961. George's best man, Clive Bate, is on the far left next to George's mother. My parents are on the right with Janet as our bridesmaid on the far right.

George and me with the children in our garden in Dorking, Surrey, where we moved from Blackheath and lived briefly before George was elected as an MP, as it was near his constituency of Reigate. Sophie (centre), Alexander (to the right) and Sebastian (foreground) in a photograph taken for George's election pamphlet.

As the MP's wife, my duties included crowning the May Queen in 1975.

Young women sitting by Trafalgar Square's fountains, sporting trendy fashion items of those days with their hippie-style 'flower power' dresses, 1967.

Feminist Germaine Greer, author of influential *The Female Eunuch*, gives a talk at Warwick University in March 1971.

Over 4,000 women partook in the first women's liberation march in London in 1971.

Women outside the Trico Factory along the Great West Road in London, striking for equal pay and rights on 1st June 1976.

'Strikers in saris': workers holding placards denouncing the inequity of the working conditions of minority ethnic people outside the Grunwick photo-processing laboratory in Willesden, London, 1977.

The Divorce Reform Act came into effect in January 1971. By September 1980 George and I were divorced.

With divorce proceedings in motion, my world turned towards work and journalism. This photograph was taken in 1978 when I was the editor of *History Today*.

Margaret Thatcher campaigning during the General Election of 1979, prior to her election as leader of the Conservative Party and prime minister of the United Kingdom.

men's magazine *Parade* in 1962), a lack of value placed on the prospect of a satisfying career and a financially secure, independent, singlehood? Maybe it was a reflection of low self-esteem? Pessimism that if I didn't marry young, all the eligible men would be snapped up? 'Girls believe that if they are not married by the time they are nineteen, they are on the shelf,' ventured a marriage guidance counsellor in 1960, using a metaphor suggesting a permanent state of spinsterhood: ignored and gathering dust. Or was it a simple case of being in love, the desire for emotional security, the feeling that I had met a soulmate, a partner with whom I wished to form a lifelong bond, and I might as well get on with it? In many ways, it was simply the expected progression – school, college or more likely, work, marriage, children, maybe work again, grandchildren, old age: a woman's life.

The route had in fact been rather more circuitous: the motive, if not admirable, then at least clear and suffused with a certain logic. I had met my husband-to-be in the summer of 1959 while I was staying with an aunt and uncle in a small village near Stroud in the Cotswolds, where my uncle was the headmaster of a boys' prep school. I was there as a punishment, excluded from the parental holiday in a boarding house in Minehead. The previous year I had been to France on an exchange with a penfriend, organised by the school. In being allocated a penfriend we'd had to note our fathers' occupations on a form to ensure there was not too much disparity between the circumstances of schoolgirl visitor and French host. My mother had insisted that I should put 'local authority worker' on my form, which landed me with a very nice family and penfriend, the father of whom worked as a baggage handler at Le Bourget airport.

While there I met Nicole's cousin, Claude, a student at l'École de Droit at the Sorbonne. He was amazingly good-looking in a Jean-Paul Belmondo way, with dark, smudged eyes, 'bluejeans' (as they were then called, as one word), and chain-smoked Gitanes. Unsurprisingly I was totally smitten. Infinitely more surprisingly, he was taken with the tartan trews-wearing me, probably because he wanted to improve his English; but whatever the reason, he took me to hear jazz and crooners in Paris cellars, introduced me to Pernod and smoking cigarettes, talked about existentialism – indeed, behaved exactly like everyone's dream of how a young French intellectual should behave, a real-life *nouvelle vague* cool, representative of the Juliette Gréco set whose style I fervently aspired to. Moreover, he had the nicest possible parents; his father was a gynaecologist with a passion for freshwater fishing, his mother the kindest of women, who would sit hour after hour on riverbanks, knitting and not talking while her husband cast his line and occasionally pulled in a wriggling fish, most of which she insisted he throw back into the river. When I left to go back to England his mother gave me a headscarf with Paris landmarks printed on it (to be worn, unflatteringly, over the hair and tied tightly under the chin in those days) and invited me to return the following summer. Claude and I parted, promising to write weekly to each other, with me secretly pocketing a discarded empty packet of his Gitanes, which I hid down my knickers next to my skin.

All went well until Claude sent me a copy of a translation of Jean-Paul Sartre's *La Nausée*. I was at school when it arrived, and my mother, suspicious of what passed between this 'foreign man' and her daughter, opened the parcel and, as luck would have it, the book fell open at a page which read 'as I entered the café, I had a feeling of disappointment in my sex organs'. The 'dirty book' was sent back by the next post and I was told the correspondence must cease forthwith. It didn't, of course. I made up some elaborate story to explain to Claude that in future he should address his letters to the home of a school friend of mine, Bronwen, whose mother thought my mother was 'petit bourgeois' beyond belief, and turned a blind eye to the arriving letters.

The following summer I returned to France, having convinced my parents that it was a school rule and I would not be allowed to take French GCE unless I had spent two more weeks with my penfriend speaking no English. However, rather than staying with Nicole and her parents and sister, I stayed with Claude's family and had another exhilarating though entirely chaste two weeks travelling to riverbanks and visiting his family in the south, since in September he was off to Algeria, where the war was still raging, to do his national service. I felt I was living a carefree, sophisticated *Bonjour Tristesse* life.

My deceit was of course discovered, and after much shouting, hand-wringing and justified anger, a punishment was decided: I must forgo the annual family holiday by the sea and instead spend the fortnight helping at Uncle Sidney's school, taking the boys blackberrying, keeping guard over them as they swam in the local lake, taking them to see the large trout farm in Nailsworth, and other such diversions.

It was there that I met my future husband. My aunt had been a civil servant prior to her marriage, and, competent in shorthand, she taught a stream of journalist trainees Pitman's – or tried to. George was the latest of that long and disappointing line, and he came to the house every Wednesday evening with biro and spiral-bound pad. One Wednesday, we talked and he invited me out to dinner. He was eight years older than me, so I was delighted – my aunt and uncle less so. Indeed, my uncle chased him down the garden path with a poker when he brought me back half an hour later than had been agreed.

In early September, I went home and back to school. George wrote and drove to visit me at half-term, earning me the interest and respect of the class sophisticates as he turned up outside the school gates in his sports car, but the opprobrium of my parents, who refused to meet him and forbade me to either.

His appeal was his difference: older – a man, not a boy – and better educated, with an interest in film and books. After completing his finals at Oxford he had dashed to Blackwell's bookshop where he sold all his books and then used the money to go to Rome for a week. It was there, lying on a hotel bed having a siesta, that he read in the *Daily Telegraph* that he had been awarded a first, and then two days later that his father Stanley, a regional Gas Board manager from whom he had been largely estranged since his parents' bitter divorce, had died.

When George paid me that illicit half-term visit, we went to the Academy cinema in Oxford Street to see Ingmar Bergman's fashionably gloomy *The Seventh Seal*. He was also actively interested in politics, though I did not realise the full implication of that until later. In retrospect I should have divined a discrepancy in our political outlooks when he showed me a green-covered publication containing horrific photographs intended to show that the rebels in the Algerian War were perpetuating as many (if not more) barbarous attacks on the *pieds-noirs* as were being inflicted by the ancestral French settlers on them. This was not the narrative, or rather the emphasis, that I had learned from Claude, who had been to the North African colony during his national service.

It was obvious to me that I had reached an impasse in my life: I was desperate to leave home but there was no clear pathway to independence as far as I could see. I wanted to be grown up. On a school trip to the Old Vic to see John Neville and Judi Dench in *Hamlet*, we had walked back to the coach through Soho, passing couples in cafés drinking and smoking. I ached to be among them, wearing suede moccasins and a duffel coat. I should have reformed, worked harder, persuaded my parents and the school that I could try for university. But that seemed a very long-term strategy and one that hardly beckoned beguilingly, and had no guarantee of success.

My relationship with George was impossible: my parents refused to speak of him, and when he sent me a present of a skirt, my mother told me that men only bought women clothes if they intended to undress them subsequently, and sent it back. So George and I decided that I should leave home, not to live with him but to go to a bedsit in Bristol, where my school friend Sandra (now calling herself Alexandra) was studying at theatre school (she later became a model for Dior and married a man from the cadet branch of the Duke of Primo de Rivera's family). I intended to find a job to pay the rent – and to go to stay with George at weekends in the small flat above the branch office in Stroud where he was living.

Armed with the key to a bedsit, which George had sent me care of Bronwen's address, and my meagre handful of money, I boarded a train at Paddington station on 1 January 1960. I was sixteen, had never cooked anything, nor shopped for food, washed my own clothes or paid a bill. I was quaking with nervous anticipation when, as directed by George, I caught a bus from Temple Meads station to Beaufort Road in Clifton where the Yale key let me into the hallway of an imposing Georgian house and, after I had climbed an elegant staircase, another key unlocked a spacious first-floor bedsit with floor-to-ceiling windows, a single bed, a Parker Knoll armchair, a large mirror over the fireplace with an unpromisingly small gas fire, a meter which took shillings, a table, and two upright wooden chairs.

II Of Slender Means in Bristol

I expect there was a kettle and maybe a Baby Belling on the landing, but I lived in so many bedsits in Clifton over the next year that I can no longer recall the precise arrangements of each one. Indeed, the Beaufort Road flat did not shelter me for long. On the Monday after a brief interview I had managed to get a job in the kitchen utensils department of Jones's department store in Broadmead, a singularly ugly and unimaginative reconstruction of the bomb-razed city. Two days later, having bought the required black dress for work, and busy folding tea towels for display, I was summoned to the personnel manager's office. There, stony-faced, sat my mother, who had come to fetch me home. I refused to go, and a quick phone consultation with George assured me that I could not be compelled to do so.

Looking back, I feel desperately sorry for my mother and her fruitless trip. But there was no way that I was going to accompany her back to 33 Adeyfield Road and the confined and narrow life that represented. So she had to return empty-handed and concoct a story both for the school and for friends and neighbours that I had been offered such a good job in Bristol that I could not turn it down, and therefore I would not be returning to school for the sixth form.

Meanwhile, the police had somehow got involved, but once satisfied that I was of sound mind, implacably determined and in no moral danger, they explained to my mother that there was nothing they could do. However, the husband of the Beaufort Road bedsitter landlady had no idea his wife owned a small portfolio of property, so she could not risk any scandal or official intervention that might alert him to that fact. I agreed as an interim measure to move into the YWCA hostel round the corner. Predictably, I found that as restrictive as school, and the enforced companionship stifling, and as soon as possible found another place in Clifton.

George bought me an Aladdin paraffin stove and I carried that and a suitcase from bedsitter to bedsitter, away from mice-infested kitchens, draconian restrictions on visitors worse than any Oxbridge college, creepy, predatory landlords, and excessive rents, until I ended up in a bedsit above a genteel restaurant in Pembroke Road near Bristol Zoo. I liked it there. The other residents were much older but agreeable and one, a man with a wispy gingery beard and a face like the first television chef Philip Harben, and who claimed he was a descendant of the great French chef, Antonin Carême, used to cook omelettes and rice puddings for me and make sure I had a pint of milk every day, while refusing to accept either thanks or reward. In addition, there was the opportunity to eat a plain-fare meal in the restaurant downstairs each evening before the diners proper made their entrance, in exchange for washing up all evening.

Nineteen-sixty was an odd year for me. I got a job in Bright's, an upmarket department store in Clifton, where I was assigned to the lingerie and hosiery department working under the fierce buyer, Miss Gledhill. It was the era of the sticking-out, short gingham skirts in the style of the 'sex kitten' Brigitte Bardot. In order to stick out in the required parasol manner such skirts called for hooped petticoats, so I spent a lot of my time thread-ing whalebones through the nylon petticoats until canny young girls (designated teenagers by then) realised they could achieve the same effect by dipping their petticoats in a solution of sugar and water and letting them stiffen as they dried – though if it rained, or the petticoats became sodden with perspiration, they must have had a sticky and uncomfortable end to the evening.

I can't imagine I was much good at that job. The only garments on display were on plaster torsos, so if a customer wanted a pair of knickers or a 'brassiere' (as Miss Gledhill referred to these doughty garments) or a deliciously slithery satin slip, she would have to ask an assistant, who would pull out a glass-fronted mahogany drawer and, wearing white cotton gloves, unfold the merchandise for the customer's perusal. However, whatever my inadequacies, the other staff were very kind to me, and gathered round and clapped when the wages clerk brought round the weekly wages in small brown envelopes on a Friday and they realised it was my first proper pay packet.

I don't know why I left Bright's. I don't think I was sacked. Maybe I agreed to leave as part of some bargain with my parents to get a 'proper job' in local government, like my father. Maybe it was because I didn't want to work on Saturdays because I preferred to take the bus to Stroud to spend my weekends with George. In any event, I found a job working in the offices of Kingswood Urban District Council on the northern fringes of Bristol. I learned how to operate a very simple telephone switchboard (with apertures shielded by what looked like blinking eyelids to plug the connecting wires into), open the post, file, and work the Gestetner machine. Again, everyone was very kind to me, too kind in the case of the chief clerk, a dusty, Dickensian, cadaverous, avuncular man who was horrified at the idea of a sixteen-year-old girl living on her own in bohemian Clifton and did everything in his power to find me digs in a family home near the office. I resisted.

I had shown some initiative in leaving home, but I showed little after I arrived in Bristol. I had hardly any money once I paid my rent and was often hungry. The tea in a stained plastic mug served with a sugary Nice biscuit every afternoon at the council offices was the high point of my day, and each Friday (pay day) I would buy a tin of condensed milk and eat one spoonful of the thick sweet confection every evening for the following week.

All I looked forward to was the weekend, when I would get on the bus to go to stay with George in the flat – or rather a bedroom, kitchenette and office with an ever-rattling teleprinter

– above the classified ads department of the *Bristol Evening Post* (Stroud and District edition) in the high street. It was then that I would eat: we would grill gammon steaks, or chops, or go out for dinner on Saturday night in a local hotel or pub.

It was a magical time: the Cotswold villages of Uley, Dursley, Painswick with their soft sand-coloured stone seemed sunlit for that entire summer. *Cider with Rosie*, Laurie Lee's lyrical memoir of his childhood in the village of Slad, the most beautiful of all the nearby villages, had recently been published to enthusiastic acclaim and he was in great demand locally (and in literary London too, no doubt) to open fetes, judge produce and craft shows, and more appropriately, give readings in village halls.

Since Lee lived on George's journalistic patch, we followed him around with the paper's photographer, Terry Garrett, and George managed to establish a fruitful relationship with the *Sunday Express* by acting as their one-summer Slad correspondent. Many evenings we would drink (cider, appropriately) in the Star Inn in Slad with Laurie Lee and his statuesque and improbably beautiful wife Cathy, whom he liked to say he had fallen in love with when she was a fourteen-year-old girl dancing barefoot on the quay in Marseilles and he was on his way back from the Spanish Civil War. We spent one evening in the Star admiring Cathy trying on hats she had got on approval from a shop in Cheltenham, I think, to wear when she and Laurie went to a royal garden party to which they had been invited. Being asked to choose the best one was for her an impossible task. She looked stunning in each, so the entire pub had a show of hands to decide as she obligingly paraded round the bar – though we never knew if she took our advice.

At some point I decided that I really couldn't stand working for Kingswood Urban District Council anymore. George had by this time come back to the Bristol office and was learning to be a sub(editor) on the *Western Daily Press* – where Tom Stoppard also worked as a journalist for a few years – which entailed night work, and we wanted to spend the days together. I embarked on the usual fill-in occupation: waitressing. First on the breakfast shift at the Hawthorns Hotel, from where I got the sack because I was too slow at dishing out the bacon and eggs, toast and marmalade, then at Horts restaurant in Bristol which catered largely for businessmen at lunchtime and middle-aged couples at dinner. The maître d' was a Mr Peel ('the name may be Peel, but I'm no lemon') and a fellow waitress was Glenda Jackson, whose then husband, Roy Hodges, was direct-ing a summer season in Weston-super-Mare. This was still several years before Jackson made the big time in Peter Brook's 'Theatre of Cruelty' project. But her fluid, straight-backed grace marked her out as special, and I watched fascinated as she effortlessly wove her way round the tables with a lithe elegance that gave the impression that she was skating on an ice rink.

It was about this time that George and I decided we wanted to get married. I can't remember being proposed to; we lived together now anyway, though I hid in the wardrobe if the off-site landlady knocked on our door. Since I was not pregnant, not much would change, I thought. It just seemed the next step in life.

Predictably and reasonably my parents objected: I was only just seventeen ('My goodness, if I had married the boyfriend I was going out with when I was seventeen ...' was a usual response to the news), and unless you eloped to Scotland (Gretna Green was the favourite) you could not get married without parental consent until eighteen. There was talk of making me a ward of court on my parents' part and of applications to magistrates on ours. But in the end my parents capitulated, my mother warning me that sex was certainly not all it was cracked up to be, though I bought a black nylon 'baby doll' nightdress as a mark of change of status.

We posted the banns for early February 1961 and were married a couple of weeks later. George went to the bank to try to raise a loan for a honeymoon in France, but was told that he needed collateral and that a spasmodically employed teenage wife-to-be hardly fitted that bill. So he bought a rakish astrakhan hat with the money left in his account and we resigned ourselves to the Jurassic coast rather than Paris. Then, having assembled a collection of wedding presents, including several Pyrex glass dishes on metal stands and Denbyware casseroles with green ears of wheat painted on the sides, we returned to the same bedsitter in Clifton that we had denied living in together before the wedding, a married rather than an unmarried couple.

Chapter Six

Spanland

In August 1961, George was posted to London so we set about finding somewhere to live. It always intrigues me how incomers to a city with no connection to a particular area decide where to settle. Obviously it is partly a matter of cost, but many London postcodes have equivalent values, and if I ever go somewhere like Tulse Hill, Battersea, Queen's Park, Camberwell, or Sheen, for example, I wonder why chance did not lead us to move there. In our case we had of course heard of Hampstead and fancied living among its leafy streets reputedly encompassing a left-wing literary and artistic culture, not realising how the Finchley Road cuts a swathe through the borough, leaving the heath rising on one side and a slow descent into Kilburn on the other. A further spur was the advice of the woman in the letting agency to which we had gone to find a flat, who pointed out that Finchley Road was on the number 13 bus route to Fleet Street where the *Evening Post* had its London office.

As soon as we arrived in London, I started a job that I had seen advertised while still in Bristol, in the art department of the *TV Times*. The advert had specified 'art school training', but I applied anyway. I got the job, which turned out to involve sizing up photographs with a red chinagraph pencil for the Grampian (Scottish) edition of the independently published rival to the BBC's *Radio Times*, in the days when commercial television was both deemed vulgar and envied as a 'licence to print money'. *Coronation Street, Emergency – Ward 10, Bonanza, Robin Hood, 77 Sunset Strip, The Avengers, World in Action* and *Double Your Money* were among the hit shows for which I chose photographs for each issue of the weekly magazine, but I never saw any of the programmes myself, as even now married and grown up, we had no television.

Our first London home was an un-self-contained flat (small kitchen and living/bedroom) in West Hampstead. We shared a bathroom where there was a geyser for hot water, meeting fellow tenants on the landing most mornings and evenings clutching towels and sponge bags. The house was owned by Mr Bard, a quietly spoken German émigré who was courtesy itself when driven to complain mildly about the late hours we kept, the doors we banged, the number of times we clattered down the stairs to answer the payphone in the hallway. Our living/ bedroom came with a double bed, covered by an eiderdown, a dining-room table and chairs and a couple of upholstered 'easy chairs'. I threw a length of yellow cotton over two tin trunks which provided storage and an approximation of a coffee table, or as the sociologist Stuart Hall remarked in a different context, 'an occasional table which has seen few occasions'. Each Saturday

I would carry a bag full of dirty washing to the launderette round the corner in West End Lane, and sit reading while the clothes swirled around, before transferring them for an extra shilling in the slot to a tumble dryer, since there was no space to hang up laundry in our small flat.

The image I associate most vividly with that weekly chore is of Saturday 27 October 1962, as the Cuban missile crisis reached its climax. I remember being sat huddled in my navy duffel coat, watching my underwear going round and round in the dryer, and peering at aerial photographs in my newspaper of hard-to-decipher Soviet ships steaming towards the US military blockade around Cuba, where an agreement between Fidel Castro and Nikita Khrushchev had led to the siting of Soviet ballistic missiles on the island. This followed the seizure of power by Castro, who had severed relations with the US, appropriated American economic assets, and was forming strong links with the Soviet Union. The missiles were intended to discourage another 'Bay of Pigs' – the previous year's CIA-backed botched invasion to overthrow Castro and regain the assets of those Batista-supporting Cubans who had fled to Florida.

The missile crisis was the most perilous confrontation of the Cold War, until, after nearly two weeks of nail-biting brinkmanship, Presidents Kennedy and Khrushchev came to a last-minute agreement on 28 October. Like everyone else I was transfixed by the unfolding drama, though without a television I relied on the newspapers and our small transistor radio to follow the action. That Saturday afternoon as the Soviet ships approached the US military blockade surrounding Cuba, I sat rigid with fear, wondering what on earth was the point of having clean knickers, pillowcases and tea towels, since the world seemed about to end in a nuclear holocaust.

But thankfully it didn't, of course, and apart from the Cuban missile crisis, I really did not feel that I was living under the 'shadow of the bomb' that was supposed to hang over our post-war lives, obliterating most other considerations – and the future. Although I took a keen interest in disarmament confer-ences, and was a badge-wearing member of CND, I regret to say that I never joined the many thousands who marched every Easter in the early 1960s the fifty-odd miles from the Atomic Weapons Research Establishment at Aldermaston in Berkshire to hold a protest rally in Trafalgar Square. Nor, two decades later, did I join the women's peace camp set up in protest at the siting of US cruise missiles at the RAF base at Greenham Common, also in Berkshire, where the protesters were manhan-dled by the police and forcibly evicted – but then broke in again. Women came and went – some leaving children to do so, since they considered the threat of nuclear war posed a greater danger to their families than their absence; others brought their children with them, and at least one baby was born at the all-female camp. A few women went on hunger strike. Nearly all linked arms to surround the wire perimeter fence that encircled the base, and many wielded wire cutters to make gaps in the fence so they could get into the base. They were not sure if they could be charged with criminal damage, as police and soldiers fought to keep them out. Some endured the mud, rain, cold and primitive living conditions for almost twenty years.

Why was I such a slouch when it came to political activism, I wonder with regret? 'Where are you now?' the Greenham women sang. 'At home,' I would have had to answer, as would my friends and neighbours. Strong beliefs in those turbulent times of protest, but feeble in action, I fear.

I New Name, New House, New Baby

By 1963, George and I had decided that we were tired of living hugger-mugger in our cramped quarters in West Hampstead. An incident in our galley kitchen when he rubbed some of the scrambled eggs he was cooking into my hair after I had said something particularly annoying – a reaction that startled us both – hardened our resolve that we needed somewhere with more space.

He had by then picked up a Saturday job as a subeditor for political copy on the *Sunday Times*, in addition to his *Evening Post* work. So, with a somewhat improved income, we set about house-hunting. We couldn't afford to buy where we were, and wanted a house rather than a flat so we could have a garden for George to grow sweet peas, twisted round a row of bamboo canes, a hobby he had cultivated while still at school living with his mother and corgi dog on Romney Marsh. My mother (with whom I was in hands-off reconciliation since she had come to think her errant daughter had done well to marry the man she had) kept pushing Hendon as a suitable location, which was why I didn't want to consider the houses for sale there, which were pretty much the semi-detached spit of the detached house I had left so definitively only a few years earlier.

This was the time that I decided also to change my name from Gillian, which I considered almost as regrettably suburban as 'Patricia'. A new first name to match my recently acquired new surname seemed to me to complete the process of severance. There was no need to do so by deed poll: I knew that you could call yourself what you liked as long as the name is not assumed for fraudulent purposes. I toyed with Cressida, or Octavia (which I realised was inappropriate) and Leonie (thank goodness I didn't), but finally settled on Juliet – since it wasn't a million miles away from Gillian. It also had a pleasing Shakespearean resonance, though I know it would have been more appropriate to call myself Titania (but think of the abbreviation!) since I was born on Midsummer's Day.

My existing friends adopted Juliet quickly, and new friends and acquaintances of course had no reason to query it. Nevertheless, it was yet a further cruel and unnecessary rejection of my adoptive mother and I know it hurt her deeply: she had chosen Gillian because the name 'sang' to her ear, but if it did, it was the wrong tune to mine. And in any case she had changed my birth name of Olivia when she and my father adopted me. I suppose it was another example of believing that my identity was fluid: I had no anchor and was free to self-identify and construct my own persona – name and all.

One day in the summer of 1962, I met my old school friend Janet (now generally known as Jan) for lunch. She was then working as an assistant on the *Architects' Journal* and had been sent to the press launch of a new Span development in Blackheath, near Greenwich, and was very impressed. Span was the brainchild of architect Eric Lyons and developer Geoffrey Townsend, who had met as architectural students at the Regent Street Polytechnic. The name Span signalled the men's intention to span, or bridge, the gap between architect-designed modern houses, which were out of reach for most people, and the conventional mass-produced houses being built by developers such as Wates, Wimpey and Barratt in serried lines to pretty much a 1930s suburban design. As the architectural critic Ian Nairn observed in 1961, most housing estates built in the 1940s and 50s had learnt little from the design of houses built between the wars: 'Leaded lights and bow windows ... The narrowest possible gap between houses and call the result "detached".'

The Cator Estate, developed in the early nineteenth century in the grounds of a grand Palladian mansion in Blackheath belonging to John Cator, a wealthy timber merchant, had terraces of late Georgian and early Victorian houses and was ideal for such development. It was not a question of demolishing houses, or even converting large houses into several flats, but of purchasing part of the spacious back gardens of these imposing stuccoed terraces, as well as odd pockets of vacant land. Lyons and Townsend recognised the area as an opportunity to build the sort of houses and estates they had envisaged, as they did elsewhere in the country in places such as Cambridge, Byfleet, Ham Common, Twickenham and, later, a whole village of 500 dwellings, New Ash Green in Kent. A total of thirty Span housing estates were built between 1948 and 1984, fulfilling the collaborators' vision and appealing to families with aspirations to modern design but insufficient cash to realise their dream, who were likely to want to live among grand houses in elegant, leafy neighbourhoods in affordable (with a mortgage) homes in a modernist vernacular.

A notable accolade came from the stern-minded architectural historian Nikolaus Pevsner in his forty-six-volume *Buildings of England* series published between 1951 and 1974. He described Span developments as 'low, ingenious houses and flats in carefully landscaped cul-de-sacs, or set around courtyards or communal lawns with friendly detailing of tile hanging or weatherboarding, a total contrast in every respect to the council housing of the same period' – or, the distinguished critic might have added, to most spec-built postwar developments.

Wherever the site made it possible, Span estates reproduced on a small scale London squares such as those in Bloomsbury or Kensington, but with lawns or courtyards boxed in by terraces of uniform houses. Although some houses were larger than others, they all followed the same design rubric. They had flat roofs and no chimneys, since there were no fireplaces, and large plate-glass windows; some interiors were more open plan than others, but all were plain canvases with no fussy details such as cornices and ceiling roses.

A key feature of all Span estates, Lyons insisted, was the distinctive landscape design planted with saplings and 'architectural plants' such as yuccas and shrubs, interspersed with hard landscaping using cobbles, granite slabs and setts. Bollards and mushroom-shaped exterior lights among the planting were also a defining feature of Spanland. The garages for residents' cars were tucked away, with visitors' parking spaces marked out of sight of the houses and shielded by trees and bushes.

Each estate had a residents' association tasked with ensuring that the aesthetic of the estate was not compromised by hanging, say, baskets of lobelias or petunias from wrought-iron brackets, or reproduction carriage lamps over the front door, nor any mavericks presuming to repaint their front door a different colour from that specified. As each house had its own small back garden too, residents could indulge colourful floral excesses behind their own walls, but to my recollection few did – nor did they transgress the rule about not hanging washing out on a Sunday. Style fascism some may call this, but most of us who lived there did not.

Tasteful wooden climbing frames and sandpits were provided for the children by the residents' association, though naturally those children soon diluted the purity of the design by making camps and dens in the bushes with bits of plywood, polythene sheeting and cardboard boxes.

We moved into the Lane on its completion in 1963. We bought a T10 house, a similar version of those on earlier Span estates in Blackheath. We would have liked to buy a slightly larger T15 but that cost £750 more; and though today you could put such an amount on your credit card, there were no credit cards then, and £750 proved an insurmountable barrier.

Every day after the builders moved out, removal lorries or hired transit vans manoeuvred down the Lane (which really *was* a winding lane, a cul-de-sac with a field and allotments on one side and an imposing Georgian house on the other). Furniture was unloaded, carried into the houses or piled on the pavement. Those of us who had taken up residence a day or so earlier peered as discreetly as we could at our new neighbours, who, judging by the cots, high chairs, bunk beds and tricycles being unloaded, were mainly young families.

Our fellow residents in the Lane, it turned out, were architects, a couple of graphic designers, an academic, teachers, social workers (senior pay grade, presumably), a solicitor, a Labour MP, a couple of businessmen, an accountant, a potter and a boat designer. We had the potential to be a proper community since neighbourly bonds were still to be forged. For most of us it was the first home of our own. No one had links with Blackheath and many came from some distance – Liverpool, Wigan, Sheffield, Swansea. All were curious, and anxious to make the mix work. The community was like a premature and dilute version of Posy Simmonds's 'The Webers', a strip cartoon of stunning perspicacity that ran in the *Guardian* from 1977.

I loved our house from the very first moment we arrived. It seemed a new, light, airy world, far from the chintz furnishings, three-piece uncut-moquette suites, heavy faux-Jacobean oak furniture and patterned carpets of my childhood home. We residents felt duty-bound to match Lyons's outside vision as much as possible inside, and though most of us moved in with very little, we borrowed each other's sewing machines and ran up curtains. Eschewing pelmets in favour of Silent Gliss near-invisible rails, we chose plain linen or folk-weave striped fabric from Heal's or Dunn's of Bromley, or Lucienne Day fabrics, which had won accolades when they were featured at the Festival of Britain in 1951, or hung white Venetian blinds which were a chore to dust. We saved up for sturdy, rush-seated lacquered Italian Magistretti chairs, rescued the scrubbed pine kitchen tables our mothers had discarded in favour of wipeable patterned Formica – at least I did.

We coveted Scandinavian birch furniture, which was not unlike the simple unornamented Utility furniture designed by

Gordon Russell during the war at the behest of the government. But many of us could not entirely disregard the charm of Victoriana – in strict moderation – with the odd cachepot holding a palm rather than an aspidistra, even a pair of white Staffordshire dog figurines, which I still treasure but which were hard to place since there was no call for mantelpieces in a Span house.

Much respected in the Lane were Kate and Geoff Holland, both architects, who had an old earthenware chimney pot in their living room in which they stuffed a huge, dried spiky hogweed (now illegal to grow) that they had found on a Liverpool railway embankment and carefully transported to London in their red Mini – a perfect complement to the 'architectural plants' outside. Every evening after work when their twins were in bed, the Hollands laboriously hacked the plaster off the walls and painted the exposed bricks white. Indeed, most of us painted our interior walls white, with an accent colour in each room – though some found it a bridge too far to move on from magnolia. Thames Green, a sludgy greenery-yallery colour – as the name suggests the polluted Thames would be – was the colour du jour, followed later by 'moody aubergine'. Or we covered a wall in hessian and bought a colourful Casa Pupo Spanish rug, or a pile rug with a design of circles and squares which owed a nod to the paintings of Joan Miró or Kandinsky, to lie on the polished herringbone parquet floor with underfloor heating. A number of us pinned up psychedelic or exhibition posters hanging from plastic strips, since of course there were no picture rails from which to hang framed prints of *The Hay Wain*, or boats at sunset or even family photographs, had we wanted to, which most of us didn't. One couple papered their downstairs cloakroom – including the ceiling – with pages from *Le Monde*, while another splashed out on one of Sanderson's revived range of William Morris wallpaper for a wall in their bedroom.

In 1959 the restrictions on how much money you could take out of Britain had been lifted. So, many couples (middle-class couples, that is, and by now, using what indices I am not sure, I considered myself to be middle-class) were taking their Austin Minis or Renault 4s or Citroën 2CVs by ferry across the Channel to France. Most of them were set on camping holidays. While some pitched their own tents, carrying them on gridiron roof racks on their cars, others, including us, booked one of the tents that Canvas Holidays pitched on attractive campsites in southern France.

We would come back with strings of garlic, blue enamel house numbers, wine glasses, carafes, Provençal earthenware casseroles (in my case, uncomfortably held between my knees in our new Austin-Healey Sprite sports car as we drove across France). So we were more than ripe for Terence Conran's Habitat when the first one opened in the Fulham Road in 1964. Its most famous early merchandise was undoubtedly the earthenware chicken brick, which was to become a symbol of what we imagined was a new domestic idiom of continental peasant cookery, using dried herbs and creating what was known as *jus* rather than making Bisto gravy to accompany every meat dish or add a ubiquitous flavour to mince. The shop's shelves were stocked to overflowing with wooden spoons, blue-striped butchers' aprons, rustic crockery, and glass storage jars for the pasta as spaghetti (other than Heinz or Crosse & Blackwell's in tins) was beginning to make its appearance in British kitchens – just like those we had been lugging across the Channel from French holidays. Habitat encouraged customers to take down merchandise from the shelves and examine it before carrying it in a basket to pay. This was a most welcome change from earlier shopping experiences when an assistant would impose him or herself between the customer and the stock and fetch requested objects one item at a time. It was a classy form of supermarket shopping, which we postwar generation had already become used to when buying food.

A year after we moved in to the Lane I had an even greater reason to delight in our new home. The previous autumn George and I had been driving to Bexley for George to interview the Tory politician Edward Heath. Every half an hour or so as we drove I had to wind down the window and throw up. This confirmed to me what I had suspected: that I was pregnant. There were no home pregnancy detection kits that could be bought from a chemist then with their hoped-for – or dreaded – thin blue line: it would be several weeks before my condition was confirmed by our GP, Dr Thompson.

Mine was not an accidental pregnancy: we had been married for more than two years, I was bored with my job and fed up with faffing around with contraception – first with condoms, or French letters as they were usually called, and then with the Dutch cap, which was only given to married women (or those who claimed to be married and wore a wedding ring – or improvised curtain ring – on their left hand), ostensibly to discourage premarital sex. Nor was the cap ideal as it either had to be inserted and lubricated every night with contraceptive gel, just in case, or one had to leap out of bed at a moment of passion and squat by the bed struggling to insert it. One friend blamed her unexpected third pregnancy on the fact that she had found her Dutch cap in her children's toy box, tossed there by the au pair who mistook it for a teething ring. But before the pill was widely available (it was first introduced to the UK in 1960 but only prescribed to married women in 1967), this was what many women of my generation used for birth control – or 'family planning', which perhaps made contraception sound more respectable. I used to get mine 'fitted' at the Marie Stopes centre in Soho Square. The clinic was influenced not only by Stopes but by the work of Dr Helena Wright, another very influential pioneer of birth control in both Britain and China, and an outspoken critic of the law on abortion.

I was delighted at the news. I wanted a baby. George, waiting outside the doctor's surgery in the car, carefully noted the expected birth date in his pocket diary. I signed up for classes at the National Childbirth Trust. My group of mothers-to-be was instructed by a muscular young Australian woman, who insisted that sixteen or seventeen was the ideal age at which to have your first baby. I demurred. Body-wise that might be true – women were presumably at peak suppleness then – but surely not in terms of emotional maturity? Or so I thought from my already past-it age of nineteen.

We lay on the floor and learned to breathe through imaginary contractions, pushed floppy dolls through stapled-together plastic pelvic floors, were taught how to pin terry-towelling nappies onto the same doll once it emerged, worried that Mothercare had run out of first-size Babygros, held our husbands' hands reassuringly as they were instructed what to do during labour – mainly rub their wife's back and tell her how brilliantly well she was doing and to keep pushing. This was a heretical idea to my mother and her generation: husbands were supposed to be pacing the corridor outside the labour ward, or in the pub downing pints, not among the blood and gore of dilating cervixes and damp, plum-coloured emerging babies and placentas.

We were also instructed to drum out a tune with our fingers to distract us from the pain of childbirth, not that there would be real pain, we were assured, just some discomfort like a mild attack of diarrhoea. I chose 'The Yellow Rose of Texas' to beat out, but this tactic was of course a con – and an unwise one.

As my labour progressed in the Woolwich Memorial Hospital and the pain became excruciating no matter how furiously I drummed my fingers, I screamed and swore and was petrified that such unexpected pain meant that something had gone terribly wrong. 'Do stop that noise Mrs Gardiner,' the male consultant said sharply. 'We've all had babies here.' Looking round the delivery room, I saw that there were only three women, including me, to two men, so knew that couldn't have been true. Eventually after a lengthy labour I was delivered of the most beautiful, exceptionally long, downy baby we would call Alexander St John Michael.

II Marmite Sandwiches

It was then and in the subsequent few years that the real attraction of Span estates was confirmed to me. Indeed, I liked them so much that we moved to three different ones in the course of the next six years.

The great appeal, apart from the design aesthetic, was their communality. Most of the houses were occupied by young families, though a few had been bought by older couples or widows who had downsized from larger family homes. The children could play together outside: there could be no disputes over territory since the space was held in common. The stifling boredom of being with small and much-loved infants all day, every day, could be relieved by neighbours in a similar position all longing for conversation over tea or coffee. As they grew, we mothers (and occasionally fathers) took it in turns to walk the children to and from playgroup, or later primary school, in a crocodile (or rather more an alligator since there were never that many of them). Or one of the au pairs several of us employed, recruiting them from another Span resident who ran an agency and was married to the man who started a funky stationery shop (now the chain Paperchase), did, stopping on a Friday for the children each to choose 6d. worth of sweets – aniseed balls, space hoppers, pear drops, chocolate buttons, sticky lollipops, gobstoppers.

Mothers carried blankets, bananas, Marmite sandwiches, little chocolate-coated cornflake cakes, beakers of Ribena and mugs of tea out onto the lawn at teatime whenever the weather was clement enough for picnics. We organised a reciprocal babysitting book, whereby you got 'points' for babysitting and used them up when another member babysat for you. Once a month we would meet to work out the points-accounting system.

At night, wires connected to baby alarms could be seen strung between adjoining houses so that if someone needed to go out briefly for a doctor's appointment, parents' evening at their child's school or something similar, her offspring could be electronically babysat. Every night, cots and bunk beds were occupied, though not necessarily by one's own children. Sleepovers were common from a very early age, and if a child woke distressed in the night, he or she could be carried home in a twinkling, wrapped in a blanket (or that newly adopted labour-saving innovation from Sweden, the duvet) to their own bed. (My daughter is still pleased to be able to boast that as a small child she had a sleepover at young Jude Law's house when the Laws lived a few doors along from us in the last Span estate we lived in, Corner Green.)

A Chinese neighbour taught those eager to learn to play mah-jong, and to this day, though we are now scattered all over London and beyond, some of us occasionally foregather to build walls with rows of bamboo and ivory tiles, collect our 'winds' and shout 'cong', or 'pong' and finally 'mah-jong!' – if anyone can remember the intricate rules.

Completed in 1959 on the site of a pig farm and a market garden which, during the war, had been a caravan park for those who had been made homeless, the Lane was the estate of which Eric Lyons was most proud, reckoning that it had 'survived' or matured as the best of all his schemes – some accolade indeed, since there are twenty-one Span developments in Blackheath alone, several of which have won Civic Trust awards. In December 1959, Henry Brooke, Minister of Housing and Local Government in Harold Macmillan's administration, dug deep into the sod of the grassy square at Corner Green and planted a tree in formal recognition of the building of the notional millionth house constructed since the end of the war, a part-fulfilment of both major parties' promise to make housing a national priority. While the Labour government had concentrated on building public housing – 'council estates', as they were known – the Tories were committed to owner occupation, erecting housing for sale.

In retrospect all that was missing from our female sociability in the Lane was a book group, now ubiquitous among middle-class women and increasingly men too, but in the 1960s rare, I think, except at seminars in university English departments. Most of us read eagerly. A favourite writer was Margaret Drabble, who seemed to have complete empathy with our situation. Elizabeth Smart's *By Grand Central Station I Sat Down and Wept* was a teary pleaser, and Mary McCarthy's *The Group* was popular. Less publicly, we read Alex Comfort's *The Joy of Sex*, eager to glean information in those days of meagre sexual knowledge. In my case, I read while listening to Elvis Presley, Tommy Steele and the Beatles, or to Kathleen Ferrier's 'Blow the Wind Southerly', or haunting melodies from Jacqueline du Pré on the cello.

I realise writing this, that when I say 'we', I really mean the women. Most husbands were out at work all day – though mine, by this time a lobby correspondent in the House of Commons, was around during the day but out in the evening (not ideal as far as I was concerned since it made reciprocal babysitting difficult) unless the House was in recess. Trying hard to do the right thing as I was bringing in no money to the family budget, other than the hugely welcome Family Allowance, I found myself at ten o'clock at night when George got home from work cooking recipes from Marguerite Patten's *Cookery in Colour* or later Len Deighton's sparky cartoon *Action Cook Book* which was intended for bachelors. By the early 1970s, I was using Jocasta Innes's invaluable *Pauper's Cookbook*, which was big on sprats, offal, foraged foods and using leftovers 'creatively'. When we gave dinner parties George would make a dish from Arabella Boxer's *First Slice Your Cookbook*, a fish pie with a splendid pastry seahorse on top, served with petits pois. Or I wrestled with Elizabeth David's inspiring, evocative but suggestive rather than instructional books of continental cookery. At Christmas my bible was Josceline Dimbleby's cookbook and the Cradocks' recipe for Charlotte Russe, snipped out of someone's *Daily Telegraph*, which used sponge fingers secured with red ribbon like a stockade.

After the cleaning, the cooking and the caring, some Span women become very adept at needlework – I was not one of them. The only things I ever sewed were a voluminous maternity dress and a pinafore. In those days, maternity clothes were designed to disguise the bump, whereas today most women don't wear maternity clothes at all, but continue in the stretch-fabric, close-fitting dresses they wore before the pregnancy. They caress their bumps with pride: the very pregnant Demi Moore was photographed by Annie Leibovitz for the cover of *Vanity Fair* with no clothes at all. Maybe we have come to terms with the fecundity of women, rather than trying to hide our bodily achievements, as was the case in the 1950s.

Most of us also went to the cinema as frequently as we could: down the hill to the Lewisham Odeon to see such entertaining films as *Billy Liar*, *Ben-Hur*, *Some Like It Hot*, *North by Northwest*, *Saturday Night and Sunday Morning*, *A Room at the Top*, *Psycho*, *The Sound of Music*, *Dr Strangelove*, *The Graduate*, *Bonnie and Clyde*, *Far From the Madding Crowd* and *Dr Zhivago*. Those who enjoyed more complex 'art house' films took advantage of the fact that these years saw continental films such as François Truffaut's *The Red Balloon*, *Jules and Jim*, and *The 400 Blows*; Alain Resnais's *Hiroshima Mon Amour* and *Last Year in Marienbad*; Jean-Luc Godard's *Breathless*; Luis Buñuel's *The Discreet Charm of the Bourgeoisie*, and so many other riches.

The men of the Lane did have their communality, but it was less than that of the women. A couple of husbands shared an allotment, one played with a local chamber orchestra, others sang with local choirs, or played tennis on nearby courts, and several gathered together in the evenings to play the board game Diplomacy with concentration and thinly veiled competitiveness. There was not, as far as I recall, much in the way of tinkering with, or cleaning, bikes or cars.

Soon after the birth of my first child, I returned to the Marie Stopes clinic. After a not very happy time on the pill, a 'Copper 7' – or coil – was inserted into my uterus by my physician, Dr Samuel Hutt (son of the communist typographer and journalist, Allen).

The mid-1960s were the beginning of the much-needed de-medicalisation of gynaecology and obstetrics – the influential text *Our Bodies, Ourselves* would be published by the Boston Women's Collective in 1971, and went on to sell over four million copies worldwide. Women were clamouring to be seen by the medical profession not as passive recipients of its expertise (though that attitude still persists sometimes, I fear, in various crevices of the profession), but as beings who have agency and intelligence and instincts worth paying attention to. The most publicised example of this often hostile debate would culminate in 1985 with the Wendy Savage Inquiry into women's right to choose their method of giving birth and to have their wish to demand vaginal births over a C-section respected, whenever safe to do so.

At the Marie Stopes clinic, Dr Hutt (who no doubt said 'Call me Sam') was right in there. His alter ego was the ironic country and western singer-songwriter 'Hank Wangford', and he even wore cowboy boots and a bootlace tie as he worked in clinic. I liked and admired Hutt/Wangford, and years later, when I worked in publishing, I commissioned his memoirs at a time when he was the on-off partner of Dillie Keane (of Fascinating Aïda fame). Wangford later came to musical prominence touring with Billy Bragg and others in support of the miners' strike in 1984. When asked for a medical opinion he was prone to say to me, 'It's your body.' Although I didn't find this immensely helpful, I hope I recognised the democratic, empowering – indeed feminist – sentiment behind this statement of the obvious.

I did not, however, make much use of contraception in these years. By 1969 I had three children: two sons, Alexander and Sebastian, and a sandwich daughter, Sophie, in the middle. I was then twenty-six years old. What on earth next?

Chapter Seven

Making a Historian

On 14 December 1965, the talented twenty-nine-year-old Hannah Gavron, an actor turned sociologist and a wife and mother of three young children, killed herself in a flat in Primrose Hill, north London, just a few hundred yards from where the poet Sylvia Plath, also a mother of young children, had gassed herself almost three years earlier.

Hannah Gavron's proposed doctoral thesis was on 'sad and lonely mothers of the working and middle classes' – a subject resisted by her department at Bedford College (part of the University of London) on the grounds that it was academically unsuitable and that her methodology was unforgivably qualitative. Yet, a few months after her death, Gavron's work was published as *The Captive Wife*, a book that received laudatory reviews.

To a generation of young women who had been brought up to believe that marriage and motherhood were their destiny and the route to lifelong fulfilment and happiness, Gavron's conclusions were a salutary shock. This was a jolt and a reappraisal accompanied by others, in more wide-ranging works, that questioned what being a woman meant. What was the connection between the biological determination and the social construction of gender? Which characteristics were innate and which were imposed by society's conventions and expectations? These questions were raised in books, including Betty Friedan's *The Feminine Mystique* (1963), Germaine Greer's *The Female Eunuch* (1970) and Juliet Mitchell's *Women: The Longest Revolution* (1984), game-changing books for many women and a wake-up call to action. Such books of course had been preceded by Simone de Beauvoir's *The Second Sex* (1949) and *Memoirs of a Dutiful Daughter* (1958) – works which are now regarded as heralding the second wave of feminism, the first having been the suffragettes' demands for votes for women.

The concern that marriage and a home might not fulfil every woman's every need was not entirely new. It had been discussed, for instance, before the Second World War in the medical journal *The Lancet* in connection with the suburban housewife who, removed from her previous close network of family and friends to a spanking new, easy-to-run house, was described as constituting a new phenomenon, the 'neurotic housewife' who, with little to do, sinks into listlessness and depression. The key analysis came in March 1938 from Dr Stephen Taylor of the Royal Free Hospital. 'Mrs Everywoman' (Taylor's composite personification of the problem in an article on 'The Suburban Neurosis') was lonely, with not enough to do once her husband had left after an early breakfast for the commuter train – significantly, taking that day's newspaper in his briefcase – and not returning until early evening. The children were at school until mid-afternoon, so for long hours, the housework finished, such women were in effect 'married' to their houses since that is where they spent most of their day, hours of labour and focus.

The very names of most women's magazines reinforced this symbiosis: *Housewife, Good Housekeeping, Woman and Home, Ideal Home, Woman's Realm*. And the articles and problem pages in other magazines – *Woman, Woman's Own* – reiterated the message. The home was a woman's domain; her vocation and avocation; the site of her pride, security and happiness, and that of her family.

Many, my mother included, followed a rigid routine of housework (as recommended by magazines such as *Housewife*) that involved wash days on Mondays, ironing on Tuesdays, cleaning and polishing the living room ('lounge') and making the kitchen gleam on Wednesdays, while Thursdays were devoted to 'turning out' the bedrooms and tackling the bathroom. On Fridays there was the shopping to do – though most groceries would have been delivered – and maybe a little light gardening or sewing.

I recall a letter to Peggy Makins, the 'agony aunt' of the weekly magazine *Woman* writing under the eponymous name of Evelyn Home, from a vicar's wife. Her concern was that Mondays were her husband's day off and he wanted to make love to her on Monday evenings. Whereas she, worn out by the physical hard labour of Monday wash day, scrubbing, pounding, rinsing, starching, pushing sheets and clothes through the mangle before hanging them out on the washing line in the garden to dry, just wanted to go to sleep. The obvious answer, suggested by Evelyn Home, to change wash day to another day of the week, seemed not to have occurred to her.

'Mrs Everywoman' of 'Everysuburb Estate' was 'nervy', racked with vague aches and pains, and even having another baby only occupied her time for a few years. She could hardly go on having babies to fill all her lonely hours, and it would not be seemly for her to seek company by going to the local pub, as her husband might have done. All Dr Taylor could suggest was that she should listen to the wireless and maybe compile a list of books to read in order to while away the hours until 'hubby' returned. However, Dr Taylor was not optimistic about a cure for the 'neurotic housewife', and foresaw years of such women haunting doctors' surgeries.

By the 1960s this problem had not evaporated – though at least the horizon of women's magazines (among them *She* and *Nova*) had widened, in recognition that 'woman' and 'home' were not necessarily conjoined. I recall that when my three children were very small, I used to look forward to the weekly visits of my cleaning lady to break up the long housebound day. I would make coffee and bring out biscuits and we would sit down to talk, which jollied me up – even though I lived on a Span estate, that paradigm of communality and conviviality.

This is a reminder that one must be wary of idealising such communities. We all know how excluding villages can be to incomers. When we lived in Corner Green, that most Arcadian niche of Spanland, a neighbour who had four children – the youngest profoundly deaf as a result of her mother contracting German measles whilst pregnant – killed herself one sunny afternoon a few weeks after her husband had left her to set up home with another woman a few doors away. None of us suspected her intention, none had even begun to plumb the profound depth of her misery. All we could do was retrospective: invite her bereaved children into our houses for tea and extend a hand of unjudgemental friendship to the 'other woman' who could not have envisaged how her connivance in an adulterous liaison would end in tragedy that would blight so many lives – including hers.

On 19 February 1960, the journalist Betty Jerman wrote a piece for the *Guardian*, which had a women's page, and was the first national newspaper to do so. The page had been started in 1922, but its most influential period was under the editorship of Mary Stott between 1957 and 1972, giving space to many talented writers such as Polly Toynbee, Fiona MacCarthy, Alison Adburgham (whose daughter Jocelyn was a classmate of mine at Berkhamsted), Suzanne Lowry and, most notably perhaps, Jill Tweedie. The headline to Jerman's article was 'Squeezed in Like Sardines in Suburbia'. Based on personal testimony, she described suburbia as 'an incredibly dull place to live', and blamed women who 'stay here all day looking back with regret to the days when they worked in an office'.

This appears a rather unsympathetic judgement, particularly from one who could afford a daily nurse at a rate of twenty-five shillings a day, though this seemed 'a small payment' since the nurse (in Jerman's words) 'bathed and gave breakfast to my son, bathed the baby, changed the baby throughout the day, washed and ironed all the children's clothes, shopped and cooked lunch, got my son to rest and took him for a walk while I slept, and returned to make me a cup of tea, prepare tea for the boy, get him to bed and prepare dinner for self and husband'. Jerman also employed a cleaner, and made use of a nappy service.

Nevertheless, her 1960 comments touched a chord with many readers including a Wirral housewife, Maureen Nichol, who wrote to the paper suggesting 'that perhaps housebound wives with liberal interests and a desire to remain individuals could form a national register so that whenever one moves one can contact like-minded friends'. The result was the National Housewives' Register, which a decade later would have over 25,000 members.

While working at the *TV Times* in the 1960s, I had a colleague whose wife displayed the same symptoms as the unfortunate 'Mrs Everywoman' of the 1930s. Her GP's advice was similar: have another baby, he told her. But for me, there was another possibility. Get a job.

I Educating Juliet

This was a period featuring what might be called the 'graduate wife syndrome'. Educated women – loving and conscientious mothers guided by the liberal but practical ideas of baby and childcare advocated by the American guru Dr Benjamin Spock – were desperate to get back to work for social, intellectual, moral and financial reasons, while not jeopardising their small children's security and happiness. Some already had had careers that they were able to pick up again, albeit in a somewhat attenuated form. A few had only taken the statutory maternity leave and returned to work as accountants, architects or teachers, hardly missing a beat. They would employ older local women to look after their children, or would share a live-out nanny (no room for live-in); or rely on au pairs who were in the country to learn English and achieve the Cambridge Proficiency qualification, and who, in exchange for living as family and modest pocket money, would help with the children and babysit (and unfortunately sometimes be expected to do a great deal more).

Apart from often having an acute case of cabin fever, I had little in common with the educated women in Spanland, most of whom I liked very much. Conscious that I was profoundly *under*educated, I would often go to the Blackheath village bookshop, pushing my older children in their double pushchair, while our current au pair (Monika from Austria, Michèle from Belgium, Daria from France, Liselotte from Norway, Britt from Sweden or Ornella from Italy) followed with the littlest one in that liberating 1960s invention, the Maclaren buggy: lightweight and foldable like a golf caddy that hooked over one's arm when getting on and off public transport. In the bookshop I would stare at the small selection of classics, poetry, sociology, history, politics and philosophy books, knowing that I needed to unlock at least some of the truths contained within, but not having a clue where to start.

I decided that, having left school with just seven O levels, the first step on my belated path to education had better be to get some A levels, and so enrolled at Walbrook College near Waterloo to study A-level history, English and Latin. My fellow students were a varied bunch. They were mainly women, though there were a few men whose careers in the military or civil service allowed them to leave in their fifties with a reasonable pension, among them several colonial servants – most, I recall, were East African policemen. Other students had for some reason missed out on completing their education. There were a number of young women, 'mature students' like me, who had finished schooling prematurely and had come to realise how restricting that was: several pupils had been at secondary moderns or other schools with limited ambitions. There were girls who had been expelled, or had dropped out from fee-paying schools, a disproportionate number from convents. This cohort also numbered the eloquent and inky-fingered Judith Williamson, who had fallen out with St Paul's Girls' School and would in 1978 write one of the founding texts of cultural studies, *Decoding Advertisements: Ideology and Meaning in Advertising.*

On the whole, I found further education an exhilarating experience. The teaching was mostly good, sometimes very good, in all three subjects I studied – and above all it was encouraging. I regained my academic confidence, only quickly almost to lose it again when I applied to university. Given my family situation with three small children and a husband by now pursuing unexpected (to me) political ambitions, I had to find a university in London, so I applied to four London colleges. My first interview was at Queen Mary College, QMC, in Mile End, part of the University of London.

I travelled to the East End wearing a plum-coloured Biba maxi-coat, which I hoped could be read as the apparel of an eager, youthful, open-minded, yet committed and hardworking potential student. There I was called into the study of R. F. Leslie, Professor of International Relations. After I had managed to translate a French text (which had thrown me until I realised words like 'aggrandisement' and 'conference' were the same in English and French) my interview began. Professor Leslie's opening question was: 'Have you had a hysterectomy?' (Trying to hide my shock, I told him I hadn't.) 'Have you got a deep freezer?' he asked next. 'Yes,' I was able to say. He nodded and continued, adding presumably by way of explanation: 'We had a married woman student here last year and it didn't work out.'

After a question about the Napoleonic Wars and how they had reconfigured European alliances, and one about the relative roles of Cavour and Garibaldi in the unification of Italy, I was dismissed.

I sloped out onto the Mile End Road shaken and near to tears, convinced that I would be rejected by all the London colleges to which I had applied. I was so unschooled in notions of patriarchy and sexism and had so imbibed the daunting idea that I was expected to carry the soi-disant shortcomings of my sex on my (then) slender shoulders, that it was some time before the full affront of these deeply offensive probings hit me. How many male students had dropped out, failed expectations, hadn't 'worked out' every year, I wondered? Yet the department continued to accept them presumably without questioning them about their domestic arrangements – or their insides. On the opposite side of the road to QMC was an insurance brokers, and for a long moment I considered going in there to ask if they had any vacancies, since it looked as though my future did indeed lie behind an office desk, as I had always suspected it would.

However, to my amazement a letter arrived a week or so later offering me an unconditional place at Queen Mary's. By that time

King's College and University College had offered me unconditional places too. I chose UCL, that 'ungodly place in Gower Street', where to this day the wax model of utilitarian philosopher Jeremy Bentham sits in a glass case in the entrance hall. But it was other features of the college that swayed me: the fact that the (very fine) chapel seemed to be given pride of place at King's, and that when I went to the ladies' loo, three doors opened and out of two popped nuns in full habits! At the time I was at the height of my rejection of the Anglican Church of my childhood, which I considered a not inconsiderable part of my 'repression'. I was firmly plodding along an unwavering path of rational secularisation with occasional digressions to go to listen to the music of High Anglicanism, or to look at the pre-Raphaelite aesthetics of places of worship such as All Saints, Margaret Street, in the West End.

I remember my years at UCL as being supremely happy, though there were incidents I regret. In 1974, Fergus Maclean, son of the Cambridge spy ring member, Donald Maclean, was accepted as an undergraduate in UCL's history department. Questions were asked in the Commons about a 'traitor's son' taking a place at a British university at the taxpayer's expense. On being alerted to this, the *Daily Express* sent photographers round to besiege Fergus as we emerged from the Gustave Tuck lecture theatre. We must all have been well aware why the cameras were there, yet none of the student body, me included, did anything at all to shield the unfortunate and wholly innocent young man from the prurient cameras.

Of the five 'mature' students, I was the only one with children. I therefore missed out on the social aspects of 'uni' – the parties, the drinking, the inter-student sex – since I had to get home to serve up fish fingers and spend some guilt time, moulding Play-Doh, finger-painting, playing rounders with my children. But intellectually it was revelatory: the opening-up of new ways of thinking, of new ideas, of new possibilities, was extraordinary.

I was taught by some remarkable people: A. J. P. Taylor, whose party trick was to bring his engrossing lectures to a rounded end on the stroke of one hour as we students hung on his every word, wondering if he would manage to do so again this week (he always did); Peter Clarke, the groundbreaking historian of New Liberalism; Jimmy Burns, whose deeply thought through and gently explained history of ideas was the most impactful of all my studies and made me a lifelong (though inactive) Marxist, since Marx's explanation of power relations and economic systems immediately chimed with me. This would probably have surprised Professor Burns, since he certainly wasn't one – John Stuart Mill was more in his line.

Then there was the historian of France, Douglas Johnson, for whom I formed a deep attachment and who was a generous opener of doors and pointer to expanded possibilities (which later would include references for jobs, reviewing for the *Times Higher Educational Supplement*, attending *New Society* parties and joining the London Library). The summit of this came when, as a postgraduate, I was commissioned to collect the celebrated French Marxist philosopher Louis Althusser from Heathrow airport in my car, a battered Citroën 2CV. I had been briefed to bring him to UCL to meet Professor Johnson, with whom he had been a student at the École Normale Supérieure in Paris, in preparation for a seminar he was to give at Senate House. But Althusser had other ideas: primarily he had set his sights on buying an old English pub piano to take back to France. So I spent the rest of the day driving him round the pubs I knew that had a piano (not many) and those which looked as if they might. Not surprisingly we were unsuccessful, so I drove him to a second-hand dealer in the Caledonian Road, where we did indeed find a fine, battered old joanna for sale, but by this time the French intellectual had lost interest in the quest.

My next assignment was to drive him to Eric Hobsbawm's house in Hampstead, for dinner. Arriving there, Althusser stalked through the gate to the front door of the house, picking flowers from the front garden as he went. Ringing the bell, he gallantly presented Marlene Hobsbawm with a bunch of flowers culled from her own beds. Clearly he had learned some niceties of social etiquette but had not quite joined up all the dots.

A few years later, at the École Normale Supérieure, Althusser strangled to death his wife Hélène, while massaging her neck. Since there were no witnesses, it was disputed whether he had intended to – though in his posthumously published autobiography, he claimed that his action was indeed murder. He was found not guilty by reason of diminished responsibility and committed to a psychiatric hospital.

I worked hard at UCL: my children were in bed by 7 p.m., so I was able to study late into the night, and the history department was very helpful, giving me permission to use a room allocated to the Bentham Project on a Friday so I could write the required weekly essay in peace. I read and thought a lot, was awarded a departmental prize and got a first – despite an apparently abominable medieval paper in which I quoted a couple of times from works and people who did not exist.

II A Faulty Turn

In those generous days of fees paid, housing benefit and student grants (with part of which I bought a carpet for our Span house, on the logic that time spent cleaning, or in this case, polishing parquet floors, meant less time studying), not to mention housing allowances and vacation loans, the Department of Education and Science offered anyone who achieved a first funding for a doctorate.

Since the people I admired most during this time were academics, I decided that that was what I wanted to be. I was urged to consider Oxford or Cambridge to do my PhD – Lucy Cavendish College, Cambridge, was said to be particularly welcoming to mature women students. But for various reasons, some pragmatic and sensible, others more fallible and ill-judged, I stayed at UCL. It was suggested that a suitable topic for me, given my domestic situation, would be the application of the Poor Law in north London in the later nineteenth century. I bridled at the sensible, restrictive nature of this. Besides, I was drawn to French political history: this was a time when Léon Blum, Jean Jaurès and above all the tragic Pierre Drieu la Rochelle were favourite subjects for theses and dissertations.

Encouraged by Douglas Johnson, I decided to research the French Communist Party (PCF) in the years of reconstruction following the Second World War, when three of its members served in government. The PCF had been a party of structural opposition before the war, and had gained great political credit for the brave activities of many of its members in the Resistance during the war. Known as *le parti des 75,000 fusillés* (the 'party of the 75,000 executed') in recognition of this, and emerging as the largest single party in France in the October 1945 elections, the PCF was nevertheless rewarded with no front-rank ministries in de Gaulle's government from 1944 to 46.

This, however, was a ridiculous subject for me to contemplate. My French was little above O-level standard and I would need to live in France to understand the intricacies of French politics and society, in addition to gaining the trust of deeply suspicious and guarded members of the PCF. Yet the best I could manage was to arrange childcare for two or three days at a time in order to read in the Bibliothèque Nationale in Paris, rather than the many months required researching in archives all over France, and interviewing anyone who was prepared to talk to a fairly ignorant English postgraduate about this still raw and sensitive part of their recent history.

Instead I spent several months improving my French and day after day peering at smudged microfilm copies of the PCF newspaper *L'Humanité* at Colindale, a dreary spot near the top of the Northern Line where the British Library's newspaper collection was housed. It was an utterly morale-sapping period, relieved only by acting as an occasional teaching assistant at UCL and by filling in as maternity cover teaching modern European history at the Polytechnic of Central London and stints teaching American year-abroad students.

My colleagues and I took these students on cultural expeditions to museums and galleries, and theatres; we appropriated (rather than invented, I suspect) an Iris Murdoch walk round London, culled from references in her novels (which included the now sadly long-gone bar in Sloane Square Underground station). We had a long weekend in Dublin, during which my fellow teachers (including the architectural historian Gavin Stamp and Dickens scholar Andrew Sanders) and I went off to ferret out all sorts of places of historical and cultural interest. We strolled through Phoenix Park, where in 1882 the British government's Chief Secretary for Ireland, Lord Frederick Cavendish, and Ireland's most senior civil servant, Thomas Burke, were stabbed to death by men calling themselves the 'Irish National Invincibles'. We visited the General Post Office in O'Connell Street, the site of the 1916 republican Easter Rising against British rule, and visited Kilmainham Gaol where fifteen of the rising's leaders were executed by firing squad. We saw paintings by William Orpen, John Lavery and Jack Yeats. We followed in the footsteps of Molly Bloom's walk round the city. We gazed at 'the sea, the snotgreen sea, the scrotumtightening sea' as James Joyce, his very self, had done. And at the end of the day, when the students were tucked up in bed, or more likely carousing in the bars round St Stephen's Green, we sipped Irish whiskey in the Shelbourne Hotel, where all the men looked like poets, or so I thought, since I had fallen headlong in love with this beautiful, quintessentially late-nineteenth-century European city.

I eventually switched my thesis topic to look at the marginally more accessible subject of de Gaulle's relationship with the Resistance during the war. Yet at the end of three years of study and research, when I should have been what the Americans call

an ABD (an 'All But Done'), I was in fact F[ar] F[rom] D[one].
I was deeply ashamed of my failure to complete my PhD, in
terms not only of weakness of resolve and character, but also of
wasting state money awarded generously and in all good faith.
Subsequently I have taught courses on Eurocommunism and I
still read as much as I can of new work on the PCF, the
Resistance, collaboration, Vichy and the fate of French Jews – in
some way, perhaps, keeping a tenuous tryst of loyalty in recom-
pense for an abandoned relationship.

But my years of formal education were finally over. It had
been a mixed bag. And now I was ready to go out into the
world.

Chapter Eight

A Political Wife

‘Sterile mirror, sterile mirror,’ chanted rows of Warwick
University students in the autumn of 1968. Sitting on the platform in one of the university's lecture halls, I was pregnant with
my third child, who would be born the following February. I
clearly wasn't sterile, nor – though they could not have known
it – was I a mirror, certainly not in the sense that the chanting,
slow-handclapping students presumably meant it: an authentic,
silent reflection, a repeating image with no function other than
a continuation of that image ad infinitum. By definition a
mirror can reproduce only what is immediately present facing
it. And depending on the size of the mirror and its position, it
is likely to provide little or no context that might give a different meaning to the image. I was certainly present on that
Warwick platform, but what I was not doing was reflecting the
intention, indeed the reality of the occasion, though my presence indicated differently.

Going along with the convention that politics was a family
enterprise, I was there in support of my husband, who was

standing as the Conservative candidate for the potentially winnable seat of Coventry South, a city at the centre of car manufacturing. At such electoral meetings the politician, or would-be politician, was there to proclaim his or her political beliefs and strategies, and seek votes to put these into practice. The accompanying spouse sitting next to him (or, much less often, her) was meant to act as a support, guarantor of integrity, and provide evidence that the speaker was anchored in the everyday, that he would understand – and indeed experience – the quotidian lives of those whose vote he was seeking. The spouse would be an extension of the aspiring MP, relied on to perform the ostensibly non-political 'soft' duties of a politician in the constituency. It was in the service of this signification that I frequently left my young children in London for a night, with a rota of grandparents, au pairs and reciprocating other parents, to dash up the M1 to Coventry, where I sat on platforms and, as the 1970 election grew closer, helped with canvassing.

Which is why that evening I sat smiling but silent, venturing no opinion, asking no questions, at the recently established University of Warwick, one of the many electoral platforms in town, village, church and institutional halls in and around Coventry. A new university in the Midlands had been mooted in 1945, yet it would be twenty more years before it was built, as part of the expansion of higher education following the Robbins Report on Higher Education, published in 1963, which found that only six per cent of young people went on to university and three per cent to teacher-training colleges, or other vocational teaching institutional establishments. Though named the University of Warwick it was in fact sited nearer to

the industrial city of Coventry than the historic town of
Warwick, and had only admitted its first cohort of students
three years before my uncomfortable evening. Yet it had already
experienced the power of student protest. Because the university
had received a considerable amount of funding from industry
– its vice-chancellor, Lord Rootes, was a prominent Coventry
motor manufacturer, and its council was largely composed of
other wealthy local industrialists – there was great debate (most
famously articulated by E. P. Thompson in his *Warwick
University Ltd*) about the purpose and independence of higher
education institutions and their role in Britain's economic,
social and cultural life.

Were places of learning such as Warwick unduly influenced
in the subjects they taught, how they were taught, and by
whom, by that close connection with industry and commerce
which Conservative voices suggested was essential in order to
grow the new university into the 'top mid-Atlantic business
school'? The Warwick students had been the first to offer
support to the student sit-in at the London School of Economics,
which among other things alleged undercover political surveill-
ance and censorship of students and staff. Yet the Warwick
students' subversion was fairly mild at the time. Their most
notable transgression had been to assert their rights by painting
the story of Winnie the Pooh on the pavement outside the
university council building, Rootes Hall. Nevertheless, the
political climate was febrile in 1968. *Les événements* in France, in
which students, academics and political activists joined with
industrial workers in common opposition to the government,
had brought that country to a virtual standstill. And uniting

political activists on the left in ways that merged domestic disquiet with authority and international political protest both in Europe and America, was the US war in Vietnam against Ho Chi Minh's communist government.

In this context it was hardly surprising that Warwick students were hostile and heckling towards a Conservative politician and his appendage of a wife. But what surprises me again and again as I look back is how insouciantly and wrong-headedly unpolitical in any domestic or global sense I was, and how utterly compliant and unquestioning. The Tory Party expected an MP's wife to be a present and visible helpmeet to her husband. This, I was to find, involved my opening constituency garden parties and fetes; walking round, stopping at each stall to buy home-made jam, hand-knitted tea cosies or loo roll covers and embroidered tray cloths, as well as buying raffle tickets and guessing the weight of an oversize fruit cake. I was also required to give talks to women's groups in the constituency. (The most active of these might have been called 'Blue Streak' like the ballistic missile, or 'Blue Band' like the margarine? Or possibly 'Blue Rinse', a hairstyle sported by many Conservative ladies? In fact, now it comes back – it was Blue Link.) I would talk about how important it was not to be distracted by other good causes, for women to throw their campaigning energy into support for the party. It also involved being instructed by the women's chair, who I recall was wearing a particularly tight pair of leopard-print pedal pushers at the time, about a suitable wardrobe for an MP's wife; attending party conferences in seaside resorts such as Llandudno, Blackpool and Brighton; going to ladies' lunches and constituency dinners;

waltzing and foxtrotting with various party officials, and letting off my frustrations with such organised activities as furiously stamping around the dance floor to 'Simon Says'. I was compliant in this alien land for the sole purpose of supporting my husband George's escalating ambitions.

So there I was as a political wife with profoundly contrary politics – much like a vicar's wife who does not believe in God, I imagine. Most of the time I was an unspeaking, smiling presence on platforms, never required to utter a word and by convention only asked the standard single question at initial selection meetings: 'Are you prepared to support your husband in his role as Member of Parliament?' Each time I gave the expected answer: 'Yes, but as the mother of a young family, those responsibilities will naturally limit my participation.' But looking back, I know there were times I did not play the role well. Once, after I had chatted to a man at a constituency cheese and wine evening, and having been what I considered most circumspect in toeing the political line in the discussion he had embarked on, he turned to my husband and said: 'Well, your wife has put the Fabian case admirably. Perhaps you would like to let me hear your opinion as our Conservative candidate.'

I cannot now imagine why I was prepared to play this frankly deeply dishonest supplementary role, although it should not have come as any surprise to me that I was required to play it. When I had married George in 1961, I had known that he was a Conservative: he had read PPE at Balliol College, Oxford, but was only ever really interested in the second P – politics. Moreover, he had been involved in a conspiracy to secure the presidency of the Oxford University Conservative Association, which involved driving to Aylesbury to secure a printing press on which hundreds of counterfeit ballot papers could be forged. The deception was discovered, and it was only the generous offices of the historian Robert Blake, the don responsible for enquiring into electoral malpractices at the university, that prevented George from being sent down. However, as a mark of disapproval his vacation grant was withdrawn and he had to wait on tables at a hotel in Folkestone to earn enough money for his final year.

My husband was under no illusion that I was of similar political persuasion to him. He knew I was a founder member of the Labour Club at school, and later, as a postgraduate student, that I joined a *Das Kapital* reading group. I can only imagine that he thought that my socialist leanings constituted a youthful rebellion and I would sooner or later move to the right like most 'sensible-minded' people. But I didn't. As soon as I could vote, from the age of twenty-one, I put a cross on the ballot paper for the Labour candidate at each local and general election, though I never had to vote in a constituency where my husband was standing. In that situation I would have abstained.

I did try to fall into line: I reckoned it came with the territory, though not all the MPs' wives that I knew did so. A Blackheath neighbour, the admirable Rosalyn Higgins, who was later appointed as the first female judge at the International Court of Justice at The Hague and eventually its president, did not thus get enmeshed and kept her career separate from that of her husband, the Conservative MP for Worthing. But somehow being a homemaker and later a student did not seem to offer the same dignified opt-out possibilities.

All this was distressing and diminishing since I knew – and others suspected – that I was living a lie: a divided soul adrift among groups of people who didn't really trust me; a constituency who doubted my commitment to their causes or their values. Friends and neighbours wondered what I really thought and considered me to be practising a moral deceit and could hardly be expected to take my political views seriously. This role-play was uncomfortable and queasy-making, yes, but sometimes it was more serious than that. When I was out canvassing one day, a man on the doorstep talked to me about 'coons' and 'coolies', and when I took exception I found myself being hushed by a fellow canvasser who told me I was 'overwrought'. I was also present in the audience at the Conservative Association meeting in Birmingham in April 1968 when Enoch Powell made his lurid and infamous 'rivers of blood' speech, a few days before the Labour government's Race Relations Bill was to have its second reading in the Commons. George repudiated the speech at once, and was very concerned that Powell's words might have a seriously adverse effect on the good relations he had established with the Indian and Pakistani communities in Coventry. The Conservative leader, Edward Heath, sacked Powell from the Shadow Cabinet, saying that such sentiments had no place in a modern Conservative Party; yet I knew that a personal Rubicon had at last been definitively crossed and that, on the other side, the terrain would prove difficult.

George – who narrowly failed to win Coventry South in 1970 but became MP for Reigate four years later – acknowledged that my politics were the polar opposite to his but nevertheless could not seem to understand how it was that I wasn't able to live my life as I wished while accepting the imperatives and pragmatics of his. He supported me both financially and practically through my years as a student, both undergraduate and postgraduate. In 1973, after he had been life-threateningly ill with bacterial endocarditis, he and I took ourselves off for a long weekend to Selborne in Hampshire, where in the early autumn sunshine, sitting in the lee of the hill made famous by the naturalist Gilbert White, we endlessly discussed this intractable problem and concluded that we were inextricably drifting towards divorce, which, with three young children, neither of us particularly wanted.

We sought help from a marriage counsellor who suggested that George had fallen in love with me because I had a rebellious streak which he found stimulating and believed was deficient in his own make-up. But by this time I was in my early thirties, and while a rebellious teenager might be enticing, I felt that he needed to acknowledge the seriousness of my views as I edged towards middle age. Predictably I had been attracted to him as an older man with a wider view of the world and its mores, a stable rock on which to clamber in order to change my life as I had been desperate to do. This was all probably true, but did not address the issue of irresolvable political differences – nor the outlook and values that were endemic in these discrepancies and which would become more pronounced and problematic as the children grew older. (Indeed, after we eventually separated George still insisted that I should take the *Daily Mail*, which he hoped would counteract my daily reading of the *Guardian*.)

Moreover, George was moving further to the right as time went on. He called for the death penalty for acts of Irish terrorism, campaigned for the reintroduction of capital punishment and agreed with stringent curbs on immigration to the UK. Though he was critical of the policy of apartheid in South Africa, he did not support Mandela and the ANC, favouring a more transitional move away from apartheid, as advocated by Mangosuthu Buthelezi; he also did not support sanctions because he thought they would be 'counterproductive'. In 1975 he was proud to be one of the so-called 'Gang of Four' who successfully connived to replace Edward Heath with Margaret Thatcher as Conservative leader, the other conspirators being Airey Neave, Norman Tebbit and Thatcher herself. Despite his intense loyalty to Thatcher, she never rewarded George with even minor office, though he was knighted in her resignation honours list in 1990. It is claimed in George's obituary that he wept himself to sleep when Thatcher lost the leadership to John Major, against whom George would soon lead a virulent Eurosceptic campaign, though two decades earlier he had been an enthusiastic supporter of Britain's entry under Heath to the European Economic Community. He became the best known of Major's disloyal 'bastards', undermining his prime-ministership and charging him with being a 'ventriloquist's dummy' operated by his pro-European Chancellor, Kenneth Clarke. For his part, Major described George as 'so convoluted, he could appear in a book of knots'.

George ended his political career ignominiously by resigning from the Conservative Party after being deselected by his constituency party for his vicious attacks on Major in the press.

He then joined the tycoon Sir James Goldsmith's ('Goldenballs' to *Private Eye*) ill-fated Referendum Party, despite the wise advice and heartfelt pleading of his older son, Alexander, a political realist. In the 1997 general election George Gardiner stood in that party's interest in the same seat, Reigate, where he had served as MP for twenty-three years. After running a ridiculous, populist campaign (including hiring a donkey that paraded round the local shopping centres with a placard bearing the name of the Conservative candidate, Crispin Blunt), he came sixth, polling only seven per cent of the vote.

Chapter Nine

Putting Asunder

A shucked oyster is a mournful sight, its rocky shell forced open to reveal a pale gelatinous puddle, the Dolorosa of the marine world, whether found in Brittany, Orford, Galway Bay or Whitstable. In September 1980, I sat in a restaurant in Chancery Lane, London, having lunch with a former lover, by then a good and supportive friend, picking at a ceramic seaweed-festooned plate of oysters, matching the lachrymose appearance of the salty crustacean with my own dripping tears. I was inconsolable.

An hour or so earlier I had left the Family Division of the Royal Courts of Justice, where my divorce had been granted by a rather bored-looking judge who had leafed through a file of papers, including 'the arrangements for the children', peered over his spectacles and approved the decree absolute. I was smitten with a profound sadness, guilt and regret. Yet it was I who had initiated proceedings to end the marriage. How much more devastating would such an occasion have been had I not wanted a divorce; had I been a deserted wife, the partner of an adulterous husband with whom I was still in love despite the fact that he had come to prefer another, deciding to discard one family in order to have a go at fashioning another?

I D-I-V-O-R-C-E: The History

My experience came eleven years after the passing in 1969 of what came to be known as the 'no-fault' Divorce Reform Act, long after the Royal Commission on Marriage and Divorce had reported in 1956 its survey of changes in divorce in the first half of the twentieth century. The MP who was persuaded to introduce a private members' bill that triggered that inquiry, the Matrimonial Causes Bill of 1951, was a woman, the newly elected Labour MP, Eirene White, whose proposals echoed the sentiments of the Haldane Society (of socialist lawyers): 'The law cannot make people love one another, or make them live together if they do not do so of their own free will,' declared White, describing herself free of direct interest, 'being myself most happily married'. Therefore, she continued, 'it should be recognised that all the law can do for couples unable to achieve or maintain a good marriage is ... protect a party who does not desire cohabitation against the attentions of one who does ... make and enforce orders as to the custody of the children ... make and enforce financial arrangements ... The function of the law should be mainly declaratory – to give public recognition to an already accomplished change in the private arrangements of the parties.'

Until the middle of the nineteenth century, divorce had been a matter for the ecclesiastical courts and canon law, and since it involved either complicated annulment procedures or a private parliamentary bill, divorce was restricted to the very wealthy. The 1857 Matrimonial Causes Act had removed divorce from church courts to civil jurisdiction and defined matrimony as a contract rather than a sacrament. The number of divorces increased from three to over three hundred in a year. However, the law privileged men over women since a husband could petition for divorce solely on the grounds of his wife's adultery, whereas a wife was required to prove not only her husband's adultery but also additional offences such as incest, bigamy, rape, cruelty or desertion. The reason for such gendered discrepancy was intended 'to guard the woman from the inconstancy of her husband, who, if free to do so, would leave his wife and children whenever he should tire of them'.

This safeguarding of the financial interests of an abandoned wife and children was the guiding principle of divorce legislation throughout the twentieth century. But of course this patriarchal caution could tie a woman into an abusive marriage, and deny her any chance of finding a more compatible life partner. Moreover, financial arrangements for the wife and children could not be discussed before the divorce was granted, since this could count as collusion. So, a wife with no independent income might launch a divorce petition unsure as to whether she would be allowed to remain in the family home with the children or what financial provision for the family would be agreed.

In 1921, three years after the social and domestic disruption of the First World War, divorce rates in Britain shot up to a peak of 3,500. The same happened after the Second World War, with divorces rising to 60,300 in 1947 (ten years earlier the number had been just 4,100). In 1923 the law had been changed to equalise positions, with women now able to petition for divorce on the grounds of a husband's single act of adultery. The unexpected consequence of this ushered in the ridiculous spectacle of the 'Mr and Mrs Smith syndrome', whereby if a couple wished to obtain a divorce, the husband only had to 'take the train to Brighton'. It didn't have to be Brighton of course, though it often was: within easy reach of London and, being by the seaside, a plausible destination for an illicit weekend with a woman hired for the purpose of giving the wife grounds for divorce. The two would sign the hotel register as a married couple ('Mr and Mrs Smith' being the favoured moniker) and the chambermaid would be asked to swear that she had found them in bed together when she took in their morning tea. However, in all likelihood the man had probably spent the night in an armchair, or the couple had passed the time doing jigsaws or crossword puzzles. No matter. This 'evidence' would serve as proof of adultery.

A. P. Herbert's novel *Holy Deadlock* (1936) parodied the absurdity of this situation which was entirely contrary to the spirit of the law. If such collusion between couples was suspected, the matter would be referred to the King's Proctor; and if found proven, a decree absolute would be refused and the unhappy couple would remain married.

This was clearly unsatisfactory to all caught in this net – including the Prince of Wales and Wallis Simpson prior to Edward VIII's abdication in 1936 – and made a mockery of the law. So in 1951 the Royal Commission on Marriage and Divorce was convened, reporting five years later. It would take the report of yet another royal commission (which was sharply divided on the matter of 'fault'), another private members' bill, this time introduced by Labour MP Leo Abse (himself a solicitor), and years of debate and prevarication on the floor of the Commons and Lords, in public meetings and the press, before in 1969 the Divorce Reform Act finally made it onto the statute books. It had been a long haul; and the matter of custody, and particularly the enforcement of financial provision, proved – and still proves – contentious, and frequently impoverishing to divorced mothers.

The extension of legal aid for divorce in the High Court in 1950, and magistrates' courts a decade later, made petitioning for divorce possible for those on low incomes, but of course did nothing to improve their subsequent standard of living. The notion of a man on a low income being able to maintain two homes made a chimera of the idea that divorce would be a clean break which would enable both parties to establish new families. Moreover, the enforcement of whatever maintenance orders had been made by the courts proved – and continues to prove – difficult, vexed and frequently litigious. In 1971, only thirty per cent of lone mothers received any form of financial support from their children's father and many lone mothers had to rely on state benefits.

Although easier divorce for women shackled in unhappy unions was one of the rights, or liberations, that many women fought for in the 1960s, and legal aid for divorce petitions made divorce possible for a greater number of couples, perhaps more than any other of women's demands, easier divorce had its problems – despite the fact that between 1947 and 1986 the number of successful petitions by wives rose from fifty-one per cent to seventy-three per cent of the total number of divorces. During the second reading of the bill, the Labour MP, Dr Shirley Summerskill, had dubbed it a 'Casanova's charter', suggesting many women would bear a heavy burden for their liberation while men skipped free; as indeed it often proved, with ex-wives taking the larger part of the responsibility and care of the children during the week, while ex-husbands were more likely to appear at weekends. 'I'm the one who has to make sure the children get to school on time, that homework gets done, insists on bedtimes being kept and television-watching time limited,' complained Jean, a divorced Islington neighbour. 'Then at weekends ... [their father] turns up and takes the boys sailing, or to watch football. He takes them out for a pizza and then delivers them home, all fizzing with excitement at what a great time they have had. No wonder they see me as a dreary nag while he represents fun and spoiling.'

II D-I-V-O-R-C-E: My History

George, anxious that our divorce should not be attributed to the long hours that MPs work (a matter of discussion in the press at the time), issued a statement to the local newspaper blaming irreconcilable differences – which was in fact almost entirely the case.

We were granted joint custody of our three children, with me having care and control. We never had an issue over access. He was a responsible parent without as well as within marriage, and never let them down, always remembering birthdays, taking them for holidays on narrow boats on the Grand Union Canal or camping in the south of France, staying in Canvas Holidays pre-erected tents as we had done for several summers when we were all together. My more modest vacations with them included a cycling trip on which we stayed in youth hostels and discovered that Suffolk wasn't flat at all. Another year we and friends went camping in Dorset, where in a field in Chideock I read the children a chapter from Stella Gibbons's *Cold Comfort Farm* every night by the light of a storm lantern as we huddled together under blankets and sleeping bags under canvas. One memorable night, a voice hollered from a nearby tent, 'If you don't stop reading that bloody Shakespeare, I'll come and knock your fucking tent to the ground, by God I will.' Which rather put a stop to that companionable activity.

But even though the divorce was as amicable as it could have been, things weren't easy. In order to allow George time with the children when he didn't have a home of his own, I volunteered that every other weekend I would move out so that he could move in to be with the children, in the largish house on a main road in Kentish Town that the children and I had moved to after our more extravagant marital home in Islington had been sold.

I advertised in the local paper, the *Ham and High*, for a room to rent for Friday and Saturday nights and I learned a lot. One was not to describe oneself as 'easy-going' since, while I had meant that to signify tolerant, some seemed to construe it as an easy lay. 'Informal', 'relaxed' or 'fun-loving' families were in reality, I found, chaotic, incredibly messy and none too clean. I ended up for a few months in an academic's house in Hampstead; and while she couldn't have been nicer, her full-time lodger deeply resented my presence and what she regarded as the intrusion into her space (a shared kitchen) with a venom so bitter that I was forced to decamp to a rented spare room in the house of a psychoanalyst in St John's Wood, which fitted the 'extremely messy' rubric.

Things got a little better when I was offered use of a spare room at weekends by one of my former Islington neighbours. Nevertheless, it was a dismal time. I missed the children profoundly when they were with George, and would gaze with envy at the families walking on Hampstead Heath, at children playing football or rounders with their fathers, or mothers pushing buggies with a small child walking alongside, imagining they were on their way home for a family tea together of buttered crumpets and a game of snap. I would wonder at what I had destroyed and why – though I knew I couldn't have gone on living a double, inauthentic life, inhabiting a daily falsehood, presenting the children with such opposing standards and such a fractured view of the world as they grew up.

If it was hard for me, how much worse was it for our children, the innocents, who had no agency in the matter, whose lives had been torn apart? Divorce may be preferable for warring parents, but it is always a hard and damaging road for the children. The mistake in our case was not the divorce, but the marriage. However, that is of no account, offering no comfort for the progeny.

On that terrible Sunday morning when we told the children we were going to get divorced, as we sat round the scrubbed pine kitchen table in the basement of our Islington house, the oldest child said, as he scraped his finger endlessly backwards and forwards along a ridge in the table, 'I don't think I want to have parents who don't love each other', which was heartbreaking. It took all my restraint not to renege on our resolution, and say, 'But we do.' The middle one said very little, but was brought home in tears from school the next day in her English teacher's car. The youngest one, who was eight at the time, said, 'I think I might be all right if I had a drum kit.' But he wasn't, and couldn't be.

Families reconfigure when divorce or death or separation rives them and children are juggled into roles they should not have to play – the older ones taking too much on their shoulders and coming to act as a surrogate parent to fill in the gaps, and sometimes even filling the role of surrogate partner.

After a couple of years George remarried. His new wife was a constituent, the chair (or perhaps by then ex-chair) of Blue Link, and he went to live in her house in Dorking, near his constituency, where he covered the bare earth in the back garden with black plastic sheeting to suppress the weeds, and cultivated that most delicate and prolific of flowers, the sweet pea, as he had all his gardening life. He also kept a rented flat in Dolphin Square for when the House sat late. Every month he would send me a timetable indicating which children could go to stay with him for alternate weekends: he would never have all three together after he remarried. So after seeing the departing two off on a train at Victoria, I would take whichever child remained to lunch at the Chalk and Cheese restaurant opposite Camden Lock for a traditional roast: it gave me precious time to talk one-to-one with a child rather than the usual family melange of competing voices.

My children were not alone of course in having divorced parents – after all, this was north London; while across Britain in 1980, the year George and I divorced, 112,000 children under the age of eleven experienced the trauma of parental divorce. However, many more couples stayed together than divorced, and of course my children wished they still had an intact, happy and secure family.

Was there still a social stigma to divorce? It is hard to say. When my ex-father-in-law was promoted to be a regional Gas Board manager in Essex in the late 1940s, he did not send for his wife, but instead set up home with a beautiful half-Indian woman who worked in his new office and whom he would later marry and have twin sons with. George's mother, Ethel, was not only understandably hurt by the divorce – though the marriage had involved endless bickering, according to their son – and financially disadvantaged, but also mortified that she had lost her status as a wife. She wore her wedding ring for the rest of her life and, I suspect, whenever possible described herself as a widow to those who did not know her story. The Church of England's Mothers' Union – to which my mother belonged – refused membership to divorced women, even though they were still mothers and presumably needed more than ever the support of a caring community.

In the 1950s, a school friend whose father's first wife had died, was deeply embarrassed by the fact that she had a half-sister, the child of that first marriage, lest people thought there was the taint of divorce in her family.

I know that with divorce I felt a sense of loss and a degree of failure alongside the sense of relief at the opportunity to live authentically *en plein air*, making a new life on my terms. Yet there were intense moments of sadness, regret and loneliness, and places I could not bring myself to visit for several years as they brought back memories of family occasions.

I don't think I ever felt shunned as a divorcee; friends didn't seem to find it necessary to take sides, though we had few friends in common anyway, given our different values, approaches to life and activities. I was never aware of not being invited to dinner parties as an unattached woman, yet perhaps this happened. I can remember only one mild slight: I had been invited to a box at the Royal Opera House when, on the morning of the performance of *Lulu*, I was rung up to have the invitation withdrawn since the friend who had issued it had realised that the box seated four and so she had decided to invite a couple rather than unbalance the numbers. Yet view the box set of *Mad Men* today, and the 1960s stereotype of the predatory divorced woman in a community of married couples, the potential threat to any marriage, is a consistent theme. Watch out for her.

After my marriage ended, I made new friends, had two serious relationships and several brief affairs, invariably with clever, difficult men. Again this cannot have been easy for the children, who had to contemplate the possibility that their mother was still a sexual being, whereas children with married parents can ignore that shudder-making vision. I imagine that they also worried that a stepfather would involve a move, and the fragile bonds of family would again be ruptured or at least stretched.

Eventually, after resisting the dubious lure of matrimony, I did remarry: significantly, at the moment all three children had left home on gap years or to take up a university place, and the emotional centre of my life became a void, as the house was no longer filled with the clatter, music and general racket of teenagers coming and going, and Sunday evenings ceased to be the precious family occasion when the children and I talked after dinner, joking as we watched television together while I did the week's ironing.

The marriage was not a wise move. So, as the circle closed, I retained that independence I had sought all my life, no matter the cost.

Chapter Ten

A Working Woman

'Graduate wives', the cohort to which I had belonged until my divorce, were often conflicted about the path they should follow: be a stay-at-home mother, pursue a career, or a mixture of the two. This last option, the one that would have best suited most mothers in the postwar years, was not easy. Even so, there were steadily increasing opportunities and some of these offered flexible working hours compatible with motherhood: for instance, there were jobs in light engineering (especially the manufacture of consumer durables, so-called 'white goods'), while the growth of the welfare state and more power being devolved to local government meant more administrative and clerical jobs for women, and eventually public service jobs such as in social work and higher-grade specialist nursing.

During the 1940s the so-called 'marriage bar' – affecting many public sector jobs, including those in the civil service, the BBC and schools – was at last rescinded, meaning that women could no longer be compelled to leave their jobs on marriage.

Prevailing attitudes, however, changed even more slowly – to judge by a Treasury memo from 1947 about the department's own staff: 'To us, married women have been "a perfect nuisance",' what with their childcare responsibilities, the need to care for elderly parents and their apparently greater propensity for sick leave. Even Dame Evelyn Sharp – the first woman in the civil service to be appointed as Permanent Secretary (at the Ministry of Housing and Local Government) – regarded women as 'unreliable', on the grounds of their sense of duty to their families, the postwar shortage of domestic help, and their regrettable tendency to get pregnant, not to mention their 'lesser financial responsibility' compared to men. They were presumed to spend the 'pin money' they earned on frivolities such as clothes, cosmetics, new shoes for their children and paying for outings and school trips. Meanwhile, the idea of equal pay for women was obviously a bridge too far, and it was not until 1970 that the Equal Pay Act came into being – and is still not fully implemented in the twenty-first century, despite many shattered glass ceilings.

When my children were pre-school age and I applied for part-time work at a photographic agency (having dealt in sourcing and commissioning photographs during my fairly menial role at the *TV Times*), hoping for mornings only, or three days a week, the reply to my application was a flat rejection, explaining that 'this agency requires full-time commitment and therefore cannot entertain the idea of an employee not prepared to give that'.

Such career dilemmas were mainly middle-class ones. The mother of one of my son's friends at primary school, who had been rehoused with her family from their Bermondsey slum to a new-build council estate in another borough, had no such choice: her family's financial circumstances dictated that she had two jobs – an early morning office-cleaning job and a shift at the Peek Frean factory packing biscuits from nine to three. Although she was pleased with her brand-new, modern flat, her life was made harder by the fact that she had left her mother, grandmother, sister and aunties behind, many bus rides away in Bermondsey. The network of female relatives that could be relied on to provide a safety net of childcare when necessary had unravelled.

In Spanland things had been done differently. As far as I remember no one had mothers near enough to help out, except in an emergency. I relied on au pairs, while other mothers employed older women from the neighbouring council estates. They would gamely push our children's prams and pushchairs to Blackheath village, take them to feed the ducks on the pond, or for long walks to Greenwich Park, spoon mashed bananas or jars of Gerber baby food into our toddlers' mouths, or serve up macaroni cheese or jacket potatoes for the older ones when they came home from school. The labour of these women (who sometimes cleaned our houses too) allowed us mothers to work, study or tend our gardens – or in the case of my friend Kate and me, our allotments, ready-planted with raspberries, asparagus and runner beans and just a hop over the wire fence at the bottom of the Lane. Or we could take pottery classes, or even have the occasional day out 'in town' to go to an exhibition, or shop at Biba, Laura Ashley, Bus Stop, or Liberty.

The answer of most of my Blackheath neighbours to the question of what career I should follow – apart from the few who already had a toehold in professions such as accountancy, architecture, medicine or social work – seemed obvious: teaching. Teaching was a job routinely suggested to girls in the 1950s (and before and after). After marriage, the hours would fit in with their own children's school day – as they did with half-terms and holidays – so several neighbours and friends either enrolled at the Institute of Education, which was part of London University, or travelled down the hill to Deptford where the socialist educators Margaret McMillan and her older sister Rachel had established the 'Girls' Night Camp' in 1911 – an open-air 'garden in a slum' nursery school intended to fit in with the realities of working-class life: the first nursery school in the country to receive local authority funding.

I Climbing Stairs

As soon as my three years of PhD study were over, I applied for three jobs pretty well simultaneously in 1979: a lectureship at the Open University, a job on Radio Four's *Analysis* programme and the deputy editorship of the magazine *History Today*.

I didn't get the OU job because what was really needed was a specialist in Eastern European history, and my patch was Western Europe. I did rather well in the BBC's interviews until I got to the final selection board, when I was asked by a silkily spoken suit: 'If you came into the office one morning and were told that you had been booked on the noon flight to Kosovo, could you be on it?' 'No,' I had to reply, thinking of my three children. Was that a sexist question, since I had explained my domestic situation on my application form? Possibly, but also a realistic one, since it was necessary to employ people who were in a position to wing off to trouble spots at a moment's notice. Nowadays one would like to think that a man, who was also a father, would be asked the same question and some would have to say that their parental responsibilities made the 'drop everything and go away at once for an indeterminate period' impossible.

I nearly didn't get the job of assistant editor on the magazine *History Today* either. By this time, George and I were living apart. The personnel officer at Longman, which owned the magazine, initially put my application on the reject pile since she didn't think that a single mother of three children, the youngest aged ten, would be sufficiently reliable for such a post. However, the recently appointed editor Michael Crowder, a historian of Nigeria, met my academic supervisor at a party and expressed surprise that I wasn't being interviewed. So I was. And got the job. (Moreover, I was doubly thrilled to hear afterwards that the personnel officer had described me as 'jumble-sale chic', which I regarded as a great compliment, though I suspect it was not intended to be.)

I loved the work and was devastated when in 1981 Longman decided that *History Today* did not fit their stable of titles – specialist medical journals, monographs, educational textbooks – and was to cease publication. The small staff was made redundant. However, serendipitously, a consortium that had been put together to mount a bid (unsuccessful) for the breakfast television franchise decided that *History Today* was too distinguished a magazine to be wiped off the face of the propagation of history, and offered a nominal sum to buy it. Longman accepted, on condition that the title would continue to be published for a specified time and that if it became profitable the company would recoup some of its investment.

Michael Crowder was not rehired as editor, and the move from our elegant offices in Bentinck Street, Marylebone, a building with a sycamore-wood-lined circular lift, to the top floor of a shabby, unmodernised building in Berwick Street, Soho, was quite a shock. The premises were pretty run down, with rented rooms in which individuals and the occasional family lived, interspersed with rag-trade sweatshops and small shops selling cheap jewellery or fabrics and 'trimmings' at street level, and a photographer's studio on the floor below ours. There were 96 stairs (and no lift) to our attic offices, where the American group the Monkees had reputedly once had their London base. Despite the inconvenience of each month having to carry heavy bundles of advance copies all the way up, the relocation seemed a metaphor for a new start, a 'roll your sleeves up and get on with it' approach. As indeed it would be.

A successor to Michael Crowder was appointed, but after a difficult and not very pleasant period, I was promoted to the editorship in the spring of 1982.

'No, no, my dear,' said a man at the London Book Fair kindly a few weeks later, 'I asked who the *editor* was,' presumably assuming that I was the editor's PA. 'I am,' I persisted, though I sympathised with his confusion. The founding editors – in harness until the late 1970s – had been the biographer and belletrist Peter Quennell (always known as PQ) and Alan

Hodge, who had been Churchill's amanuensis when he was writing his *History of the English-Speaking Peoples* and was credited with coming up with reputedly, if debatably, the shortest sentence in the English language, 'Time passed.' I must have seemed to my inquisitor a considerable let-down from those dizzy social and literary male pinnacles.

But for me it was an exciting time. We were a small staff – all women as it turned out – and though our owners took responsibility for the business side of things and took an active interest in the magazine's content, we dealt with everything else: commissioning and editing; choosing the illustrations; production; distribution; subscriptions; advertising. And we went down the 96 stairs and round the corner to Poland Street to do our photocopying, and then trudged up the 96 stairs again.

We had a party every Christmas in the office, with paper chains round the filing cabinets, and the staff wearing feather boas instead of name badges. We were delighted at how many people were prepared to make the mountainous ascent, but worried about the equally long descent after several glasses of wine with just a handful of crisps or Twiglets to eat, so a member of staff was positioned on each landing as the party came to an end, in order to catch, or at least cushion, anyone who tripped. Thankfully no one ever did.

II Rewriting History

My years at *History Today* were an education in themselves. Initially, the magazine was run as an old boys' network. PQ and

Alan Hodge had assembled such a distinguished cast of historians in the early days – Hugh Trevor-Roper, Alan Bullock, Asa Briggs, A. J. P. Taylor among others – that they only had to see what came through the letterbox to be able to assemble an interesting issue of the magazine each month. If that fell short, they could pick up the phone and ask their stalwarts what they were currently writing and if they could please squeeze an article for *History Today* out of their present preoccupation.

However, since neither editor ever seemed to leave the office (except for long lunches), they appeared largely unaware of the seismic shifts that had taken place in the study of history, and the magazine was fast becoming (if it had not already become) outdated and irrelevant. Indeed, before I was invited for an interview, I, as a keen history student and peruser of historical journals, had never come across the magazine, and had to rush to the London Library to skim through several years' issues. It had, in short, become more of a society than a social and political history magazine. And it had a strong streak of connoisseurship and a penchant for eighteenth-century European royalty, aristocracy, magnificent palaces and grand country retreats.

Meanwhile, since the 1960s, the breadth of historical studies had been expanding exponentially: they had not only a political purpose to document the lives of the rich and powerful, but also an urgent desire to excavate the experiences of the voiceless of history, those who left few traces in the written record other than the registration of their birth, marriage and death – the poor, women, artisans, immigrants. As E. P. Thompson, author of the highly influential 800-page doorstop of a book, *The Making of the English Working Class*, first published in 1963, famously wrote, his mission was 'to rescue the poor stockinger, the Luddite cropper, the "obsolete" hand-loom weaver, the "utopian" artisan, and even the deluded follower of Joanna Southcott, from the enormous condescension of posterity'.

This was 'history from below'; bottom-up rather than top-down history, with an interest in working men and women, studies of mobs and riots, of popular entertainments, jokes and rituals; in the material conditions of people in the past; in customs and beliefs. And it fitted in with the 'democratic turn' that had followed the introduction of the welfare state with its redistributive policies. It was influenced by linguistics, physical geography, sociology and anthropology, as well as by the French Annales school of historiography, which saw historical change as best explained by considering social history as a process of *longue durée*, of structural change rather than short-term events, in which social circumstances were linked to, and often explained, the changing *mentalité* of a group or community.

In the early 1980s this approach was exemplified by Emmanuel Le Roy Ladurie's newly translated and best-selling *Montaillou* (1975), a vivid micro-history which explored in great detail the lives of peasants in a small commune in the Languedoc between 1294 and 1324; or Carlo Ginzburg's *The Cheese and the Worms*, detailing the life and beliefs of Menocchio, a miller from Montereale in Italy, who was burned at the stake in 1599 for his heretical views. Like *Montaillou*, the forensic examination of Menocchio and his fellow villagers was made possible by transcribing the detailed notes taken by members of the Inquisition seeking to 'cleanse' the Roman Catholic Church of apostasy and heresy by torture and incineration.

Material that had often been considered suspect, unreliable or 'biased', peripheral and of a purely individualistic nature and interest, such as diaries, letters, pamphlets, scribbled notes, scraps of laundry and shopping lists and perhaps above all oral testimony, interviews and recorded conversations, was increasingly woven into the historical narrative, which would change its focus to bring a greater empathy, vividness and humanity to social history. Now history could reach far beyond the classroom or the seminar space, recounted with such richness, such insights into daily lives and motivations, that the best might read like an enthralling novel.

As editor of *History Today*, I was determined to pick up on these new developments, which ran parallel to the intentions of the magazine: to make academic history readable and interesting to those with no particular specialist knowledge, but who had maintained a fascination with the past. Perhaps they had read history as students and were now teaching or in the civil service, working as administrators, planners or policy wonks, as indeed our readership surveys showed they were, though one survey also revealed a greyhound trainer who had been a reader since the off. While ever mindful of the need to keep the magazine's loyal subscribers on board with the sort of articles they enjoyed reading, we needed to reach out further to vivify and extend the contents of the magazine and bring the exciting new horizons of history to a wider audience.

I visited British and Irish universities with interesting-sounding history departments and corresponded with historians from the United States, Australia and other parts of the world. I went to conferences at home and abroad to try to pick up the drift of current scholarship and work out what would translate into articles for the magazine. Almost everywhere I received a warm welcome and found that scholars were anxious to disseminate their work to a wider audience.

In 1982 I attended a conference at the University of London on 'Blacks in Britain' and was so absorbed by this shamefully largely ignored rich history that I commissioned articles from a number of those giving papers, leading to a special issue on the subject, with some magnificent illustrations sourced by my art editor colleague, Jacky Guy. This proved a sell-out, as did a thirteenth issue on Elizabeth I, though the staff reasonably complained that it was tough enough producing an issue of the magazine every month and they would down tools if I tried to make it a baker's dozen again.

As the first female editor of the magazine, I was particularly conscious of my duty to female readers and historians. By this point, the word 'women' was ceasing to be an entry in indexes, as women were increasingly considered codeterminants with men in the historical narratives and could not therefore be bunched together as a category. Sexual behaviour and proclivities, the role of emotions and of memory, the history of childhood and 'affective relationships', were being interrogated and made vivid for the general reader.

Women themselves, moreover, were becoming more prominent as authors of history. Of course a few, such as Alice Clark, Barbara Drake and Joan Thirsk had, from the late nineteenth century onwards, written history books, while the women's suffrage movement had produced a series of histories by activists such as Sylvia Pankhurst and Ray Strachey, anxious that the movement's achievements and its antecedents should not be taken for granted or brushed under the carpet.

Now, however, there was a new momentum. During the 'second wave' of feminism in the late 1960s and 70s, women had begun to re-examine the historical record, since standard texts still often hardly made mention of them. Looking at the home and workplace through women's eyes, they started to reconfigure the way in which questions were asked and history was written, arguing that family structures and dynamics, emotional support and concerns, were every bit as important as waged work and political systems; that perceptions, explanations and chronologies were gendered.

By the time that I was editing the magazine, the voices of women historians had become more prevalent, and I was pleased to give writers such as Linda Colley, Stella Tillyard, Lyndal Roper and Natalie Zemon Davis space in the publication. They in turn had their effect on me. It seems strange now that, until this point, feminism had largely passed me by. During my years at UCL, I had begun to move among the intellectual vanguard, but it still remained largely a male cohort, whose main concerns of global political and military conflicts made socialism more crucial than feminism in their view. Such men believed that they treated women as equals (except when it came to who should serve the tea and make the sandwiches after a meeting), but they were not particularly preoccupied with women's concerns. However, by the 1970s, I became aware of a band of men, many of them academics working at newer universities, who were sympathetic to women's views and demands to be taken seriously, and for whom women's concerns were more central to their work and consciousness. And at the same time, I was increasingly aware of the restrictions still governing my own life as a woman.

As a single working mother I looked for solidarity in the stories of other women who had fought for their freedom and independence, escaping unsatisfactory domestic situations. It was my personal need to think harder about 'Women's Lib' that took me to Sisterwrite bookshop in Upper Street, Islington, where I attended a series of talks by speakers who exhorted the audience to ameliorate the power of patriarchy whenever and wherever they found it. Some of these talks seemed too removed from my own daily concerns to convince me.

It took me too long to claim to be one, but I now consider myself a committed feminist. My journey to intellectual adulthood had been too chaotic to identify with any position. I was filled with relief that my daughter's life as she entered adulthood looked so much freer than mine had done. And I gained confidence from the women I met that I had the right to ask for more than my mother had asked for: to seek happiness in work, motherhood and love, sometimes exhausted by their competing demands, but often pleased and amazed that life was offering so much more than I could have expected in those grey postwar years.

Epilogue

It was the clattering of heels going past the window in the early morning that struck me hardest: high heels, sensible lace-ups, steel-tipped boots. All sounded efficient, urgent; above all purposeful. I couldn't see who was wearing the footwear as the blinds were still down, but I thought of those hurrying to work, nurses on the ward, shop workers anxious to tidy their stock, lawyers gathering their papers, striding into court, teachers making sure their students knew the classroom door would soon swing open and it would be prudent to sit at their desks. Sometimes the clatter would speed up and I would guess that the person was late, hurrying to catch a bus or a train. Then the beat would slow down, as the walker stopped to chat, read a notice, or peruse the contents of a kerbside skip; but soon the clip-clopping would start again, echoing into the distance.

Lying in my living room at home in a hospital bed, the purposive resonance of those clattering shoes, the like of which I knew would never again signal my former busy, active life, seemed emblematic of how I had lost my purpose, and posed the overwhelming question of how would I, could I, find another?

Just over a year earlier, in May 2012, I had been diagnosed with having a glioblastoma multiforme (GBM): the most aggressive malignant primary brain tumour. GBM is a rare disease, with an incidence in Europe and North America of around 2–3 cases per 100,000 people per year. About thirty-five per cent of those diagnosed with GBM die within one year, while five per cent survive five years.

The diagnosis had come as an earth-shattering shock to me – and indeed the neurosurgeon who had performed the surgical biopsy at St Bartholomew's Hospital in London was surprised too.

I had first exhibited symptoms of a neurological problem a few days before the previous Christmas, when I noticed that I kept dropping things from my left hand as I prepared the food for some neighbours expected for a drink and a mince pie. I could not believe this could be anything serious and planned to mention it to my GP in the New Year. However, a doctor friend of my daughter advised me not to delay but go to the local A&E department straight away. The result was that I spent most of Christmas Day that year in the Royal London Hospital with what the doctors thought was probably a TIA (transient ischaemic attack), a short-lived mini-stroke which sometimes precedes a more serious, life-threatening one.

But it wasn't, and from then until April 2012, between going back to the Royal London Hospital, where the neurologist considered that I probably had a vascular problem, 'certainly not anything nasty like a brain tumour', I lived my normal life, largely forgetting about the neural problem, going to stay in my house in France for Easter, where I drove around, visiting friends and pursuing my passion for going to *brocantes* and *vide-greniers*, buying French enamelware, street signs and house numbers and keeping a lookout for another blue metal 'Chocolat Menier' advertising plaque to replace the one I had rashly given my daughter. In fact, I felt so entirely well that I considered not keeping the neurologist's appointment on the grounds that it was a waste of time.

But then, when filming a television series in Morecambe (the seaside resort in Lancashire which in the 1930s was a favoured destination for workers during 'Wakes Week', when all the factories ceased production), I woke up one morning in Oliver Hill's magnificent Art Deco Midland Hotel to find that my left hand was completely alien. I couldn't control it sufficiently to put in my contact lenses, do up my bra or hook in my earrings.

After that, things moved fast. I was given a series of tests back at Barts which ruled out a vascular diagnosis and culminated in a biopsy with a small hole cut in my skull by a skilled neurosurgeon, careful to minimise any damage to my brain tissue. The aperture was stapled together for a couple of weeks while the sample was analysed. The result was slow to arrive, and when it did, I was totally stunned. My daughter Sophie was with me when the brisk old-school oncologist told me: 'What you have is very serious and people die of it. But luckily your tumour is very small and you are healthy.' He recommended that I start an immediate and intensive course of radiotherapy and chemotherapy.

As soon as we left Barts, Sophie cancelled the meeting she had planned and came with me to the BBC where I was making a series of programmes for Radio Four on 'The History of the Future'. It had been intended that I would interview an academic at the University of Aberdeen down the line from the studio. However, we couldn't make contact (and subsequently learned that he had fallen over in the university car park, hit his head, and was suffering from concussion). Sophie and I went out to lunch. She told me that whatever happened she and her brothers would be 'with me all the journey', which indeed they profoundly have been in their various ways.

I tried to let the news sink in. But it wouldn't. How can you feel perfectly well and active with plans and duties for the future when you wake up in the morning and by coffee time learn that you are likely to have a life expectancy of perhaps a year or fifteen months (I was not told that, but did what everyone surely does, against medical advice, and looked up the prognosis on Google)?

That evening, I went in a daze to the theatre with friends and told myself that I was still the same person, but with an incurable illness (the tumour was inoperable as it was in an 'eloquent' part of the brain), and that that was how I would live for as long as I had left.

The next months were a blur of shock: total despair, weeping, lecturing myself, acute anxiety, dependency, fleeting thoughts of suicide while heavy lorries thundered past as I stood on the kerb waiting to cross the road. I had daily radiotherapy for six weeks with what looked like a white fencing mask clamped over my face to keep my head as still as possible while skilled radiologists directed the beam with millimetre precision at the tumour. At the end of the six weeks I was offered the mask to take home, since it was customised to my precise specifications and radiotherapy cannot be given for more than one course. It was a trophy I had no conceivable desire to treasure, though I would come to be very grateful for its efficacy.

Still stunned, I sought a second opinion privately and was told that the combination of radiotherapy and temozolomide (the only chemotherapy drug that can get through the blood–brain barrier) was the 'gold standard treatment' for brain tumours, though of course there could be no guarantees as to its effectiveness.

I lost two stone in weight and was frivolously pleased as I slipped into size 12 or even size 10 clothes in changing rooms. I was less pleased when a skirt I hadn't worn for some time fell to the floor over my newly slender hips as I was paying my bus fare and the man behind me graciously bent down and helped it back on to me. My hair thinned and grew fragile and bushy like a duckling's arse where the radiotherapy had been administered.

I endured the will-sapping side effects of chemotherapy taken at home in tablet form. I recall watching the opening ceremony of the London 2012 Olympics and vomiting throughout. I needed a couple of blood transfusions when my white and then my red blood cells dipped alarmingly low and my limbs turned blotchy, blue and bruised. I had several short stays in hospital and marvelled at the kindness and efficiency of the desperately overworked, understaffed and underpaid doctors, nurses and assistants, and the terribleness of the food with no fresh vegetables or fruit. I bought a wig, had it expertly styled and wore it for a few weeks, but though others admired my full and glossy mane, I felt I had lost my identity in those synthetic fibres and preferred to wear a man's trilby hat over the wispy strands of my own hair.

I sought a 'new normal', a way of managing this alien terrain where all the markers were the same yet nothing felt stable anymore. I tried seeing a psychologist but our conversations made me feel worse with every visit. With Sophie I travelled for a surprisingly calm and uplifting week at the Penny Brohn Centre near Bristol, which is devoted to helping people to live with cancer as well as possible.

I tried and failed to practise mindfulness, growing tense every time I tried to acknowledge painful thoughts and then to imagine them on a leaf slipping away down a river. I went to Maggie's Centre, a project by the architect Charles Jencks inspired by his wife, the artist Maggie Keswick, who had wanted to provide a tranquil and aesthetically uplifting environment for those suffering from (or living with, as the preferred phrase is) cancer. Though I know such refuges and activities are an enormous help and support to many people, they made me feel I was being characterised and defined by my cancer. I wanted to spend time with people with whom I had other bonds – of love, friendship, shared interests, aesthetic taste, humour – rather than the restraining bonds of cancer. I only wanted to hear from friends who knew *me*, or from expert medical staff who knew the vagaries of the disease.

Indeed, I didn't tell many people of my diagnosis. This was partly for professional reasons. As a freelance writer, I didn't want people to stop asking me to write articles or appear on radio and television programmes. I needed the money and craved the stimulus, the deadlines, the fleeting company of others intent on the same objective.

A few people have occasionally charged that I was in denial, but I reject that label as I rejected the soubriquet 'battling with cancer'. I have had no option but to accept that I am terminally ill. Being in denial means simply refusing to think about something which no amount of thinking or talking about will make go away. All I can do, all anyone can do, in the case of serious illness or bereavement, is deal with it. There is no other side to come out of for me. But while I am here I can watch the leaves turn golden, drop, and then return fresh green, urgent and full of life; watch my children change jobs, move house, travel abroad; be moved, often to tears, by the sheer sweetness of my six grandchildren as they learn to crawl, walk, talk, question, imagine. I hang on in there.

I feel like throwing something at the radio every time anyone says confidently, 'We are all living so much longer now.' Who is that 'we', I wonder, as I obsessively read obituary pages and envy those who survive into their nineties and mourn those who die after a lesser lifespan than I am enjoying. I feel a gut-wrenching sadness for those I know who travelled part of the way with me, and then fell by the wayside leaving a terrible hole in their young children's and their partner's lives.

I decluttered my house – up to a point, with the help of friends – one of whom was persuaded to let me keep my yellow Dr Martens which we both knew I would never wear again. No one could call to see me without being asked to edit my cutlery drawer, itemise my brogues, cull my collection of eighteen mascaras. I tried to boost my immune system by eating healthily most of the time – kale and blueberries, porridge and nuts and seeds, lentils and beans. I took mild antidepressants, talked to those I love and delighted in their visits, and I walked and walked and walked as though if I walked far and fast enough I could outpace my tumour, win the race.

Until, that is, I had a violent epileptic seizure in France, and was hospitalised there. When I got back to London, I was in hospital for a fortnight, so weak that I couldn't stand up and had to be taught how to walk again, to remember where my left foot was. While I was away, rails were installed in my house so that I could go up and down stairs, the seats of my armchair and toilet were raised, a rising seat was installed so I could bath and shower, outdoor steps were turned into ramps where possible. I was issued with a panic button which would summon paramedics if I fell. Carers came twice or three times a day for six weeks to help me wash, and make me lunch and cups of tea. All this at no cost to me but provided by the statutory generosity of Hackney Social Services, who must have enormous calls on their resources.

A good friend from university days became a between (his) marriages lodger. He shopped, arranged theatre outings and picked me up when I fell over during another seizure, when my arms were too weak to haul myself up again. Still I maintained the charade: that I had hurt my leg falling off a wall while showing off to my grandchildren. True, but subsequent to an epileptic fit.

An adjustable hospital bed was provided and moved to the downstairs living room so that I had no need to attempt the stairs. It was here, on the frequent occasions that I woke in the night and could not get back to sleep, that I read the finest book about cancer imaginable: the Pulitzer prize-winning *The Emperor of All Maladies: A Biography of Cancer* by Siddhartha Mukherjee, 'a chronicle of an ancient disease that has metamorphosed into a lethal shape-shifting entity imbued with such metaphorical, medical, scientific and political potency that cancer is often described as the defining plague of our generation'. And I realised that the jacket carried a drawing of a crab: my birth sign, Cancer. Hardly a portent, but oddly troubling. It was here, in a hospital bed in my living room, that I noted the clicking and clattering of the feet of passing pedestrians. Here that I contemplated my future.

I am a historian. I earn my living writing history or teaching and lecturing about history or editing others' writing about history, and I have for most of my adult life. To do that I need sources: archives, record offices, libraries.

Since I write social and cultural history about twentieth-century Britain I have travelled the country from the Orkneys (the most heavily defended part of Britain during the Second World War) to Cornwall (the least defended), to the abandoned USAAF airfields of East Anglia, built when the US entered the war in 1942. I have trawled archives from Glasgow Central Library to the South Wales Miners' Museum in Port Talbot and the university libraries of Birmingham, East Anglia, Essex, Exeter and Warwick; from the Museum of London and the London Metropolitan Archives to the Mass Observation Archive at the University of Sussex; from the Oxfordshire Local History Centre to the Bodleian; from Churchill College, Cambridge, to the BBC Archives at Caversham. To the home in East Finchley of a then ninety-eight-year-old woman who worked for the Ministry of Food during the Second World War, and, while her husband was fighting in the Western Desert, had an affair with her brother-in-law, 'since everyone had affairs in the Blitz. It had nothing to do with my marriage. I still loved Jack [her husband] and longed every day for his safe return.'

I would spend hours in the British Library and the London Library. I visited galleries and exhibitions of surrealism, modernism, the paintings of war by members of the War Artists' Advisory Committee, orchestrated by Sir Kenneth Clark, the youngest-ever director of the National Gallery. I travelled to Chichester to see the work of William Roberts – 'Britain's only Cubist painter' – and to the New Forest to catch that of Evelyn Dunbar whose speciality was painting members of the Women's Land Army. I travelled to Cambridgeshire to find out about the 'Bevin Boys' from a man who had been one; I spoke to people who had been active in the Communist Party of Great Britain in the 1930s and several who had joined the International Brigades to fight for the Republicans in the Spanish Civil War. I went to visit firemen and those who had worked in Civil Defence or the WVS during the Second World War, who had witnessed sights they could never forget and were reluctant to talk about. All in search of letters, diaries, oral histories, memoirs, newspapers, privately published local history booklets, cartoons and photographs, to fashion as authentic, persuasive and vivid a picture as possible of the years I was writing about.

I would stay with friends and sometimes with friends of friends, in the dormitories of YHA hostels, in scuzzy B&Bs.

During the mainly grey and damp summer of 2010, I bought a red-and-white tent with a cross of St George on one side, which was going cheap after the England football team had been knocked out of the World Cup, and pitched it on the nicest campsites I could find near to whatever archive I needed to visit. In the evenings, weather permitting, I would sit under pine trees or spreading oaks with a glass of wine organising the material I had gathered during the day, planning my next assault on printed and handwritten sources. Often, realising that the England tent was mine, I was offered a can of lager and a packet of crisps by fellow campers – football fans who thought I was one of them, applauding my loyalty to a defeated side.

But those foraging expeditions were now no longer possible. I had limited mobility, was somewhat unsteady on my feet and liable to stumble and fall. I tired more easily and had much less energy than ever before. I was unable to complete the book I had been commissioned to write about the home front in the First World War, which had to be done at speed if it was to be published in 2014, on the centenary of the war's outbreak. Nonetheless, I very much wanted to write another book· I couldn't think how I would want to live without a writing project, and my agent and publisher generously agreed to wait.

I decided that I had to be my own source and resource. I would use material in filed-away diaries, letters, cuttings and writings, and conversations with friends who had been there, and of course my own recollections of those years. I did not feel I could write an autobiography: my life was too minor, too uneventful for that. Rather, I wanted to entwine my experiences with events, movements and changes in the wider world. My intention was to write a memoir – of necessity a fragmentary memoir – of the trajectory of my life from the end of the Second World War to the 1980s, years which I consider transformed the landscape of women's lives in unprecedented ways.

How can historicising individual lives (in this case mine) enable a historian to make general statements about a period? Everyone has her or his own story and at the same time is part of history. Lives consist of public concerns and personal issues and the interconnection between the two. How can these be disentangled or alternatively fused to make any general statements about the past? Are historians condemned to run on parallel lines between the documented factual and a collage of individual experiences and perceptions that may only rarely coincide – or collide? In any case, individual experience is exactly that: contradictory, conditioned by past experiences, by individual circumstance, by prejudice and disposition. In effect everyone comes to an understanding of the past burdened by the baggage of the past. It cannot be other.

We know we are observers of events but we are also participants in them to the extent that we appropriate them within our own narratives, which then inform and condition our understanding and telling of past, present – and future – events. We historicise our own lives and cannot fail to make ourselves the centre of our narrative, even when that is not explicit, since the optic is ours no matter how we try to site – and cite – our perspectives in a larger historical understanding.

As a historian of the twentieth century, I have reflected on people and events that affected me, as they appear archetypical, or at least exemplary, of a perception I have of the historical

moment. My taxonomy could not be other than an account of
what has impacted on me, embedded and supplemented by
what I have researched, read, heard, discussed and argued both
in writing history and in simply living.

Of course this does not in any way privilege my historical
account over any other memoirs or the hundreds of diaries,
letters and interviews deposited in archives that I have read as
the primary sources for my writing in an attempt to capture the
historical moment and what mattered to those living it. History
is not a jigsaw, waiting for missing pieces to be dropped in to
one day complete the picture, since the shape of the absence as
well as the presence may well have changed. Nor is it a kaleido-
scope, since it is the viewer who shifts, not the past.

Now that the book is written, I am struck by the episodic
nature of my life. This is partly the result of memory: you do
not remember sequentially, and so many memories are memories of memories, misleading us as we look down the darkening
tunnel into the past. But I think that my life has been more
fragmentary than most, because the world I grew up in seemed
so far away from the world I married into, which itself became
distant when I embarked on my university education and began
a career of my own. In all of these worlds I felt an outsider,
though it may not have been apparent to those around me.
Perhaps this all goes back to being adopted: to my childhood
fantasy that somewhere there was an intellectual, confidently
middle-class home where I might have thrived. Certainly as the
wife of a Tory MP I continued to think that the real world – the
one where I'd fit in – awaited me elsewhere. If I found this at
all, then it was through my studies at UCL and the jobs that

followed. But even here, though I might have looked to those around me like a successful professional, and though I found real intimacy with family, friends and lovers, I could never have identified a cohort where I easily belonged.

I think now that this was what made me well suited to the work of a historian, making me a natural observer of the lives of others. As a social historian, I've been endlessly curious about the detail of how different people lived in the century of my birth, and I've wanted to defamiliarise the lives of my subjects as I seek to understand the structures determining them.

Before I started this book, I hadn't thought much about my childhood for some time. After my parents had died and I'd created a more congenial family of my own, I preferred to forget about the boredom and claustrophobia of that house where I sat lining up my postcard collection, waiting to escape. I think now that it may have been the sound of the heels clattering outside my window that reminded me of those years when life seemed to be taking place elsewhere; when other people appeared to have the excited expectation of wishes acted upon and fulfilled, while I had merely the repetitive progression from lunch to tea, with only the field beside the house to escape to.

Yet this isn't the whole story, because I can in fact escape, even on the days when I'm unable to leave my room. I can escape now as I could then into books, and into the excitement of imagining and reconstructing other people's lives. Now when I lie listening to the heels clip-clopping outside the house, I remind myself that there's more space left to move around in than I sometimes fear. Writing this book has made me appreciate that my life has taken me to so many places, none of which

I could have predicted as I lay daydreaming in that field by the old railway line in adolescence. Then I had no idea what the world looked like. Now I can roam freely across decades and continents in my head. I'm grateful that I've had the chance to return to all those moments and places as I trace the pattern formed by the dots of my fractured memories. The picture that emerges is a messy one, but as a historian I'd expect nothing less.

Acknowledgements

It is usual for an author to say that he or she could not have written their book without the help and support from a number of people. In my case this is particularly true: without the help, support and encouragement of the people mentioned below I could not have written this book.

I start with my late and much-missed agent, Deborah Rogers, who suggested that as I had written several books with the voices of others spatchcocked together, perhaps now was the time to find my own voice; and fortunately Georgia Garrett, Deborah's successor, encouraged me to do so, as did Arabella Pike, the Publishing Director at HarperCollins.

Kate Johnson has proved to be a meticulous and knowledgeable copyeditor. I am very pleased to be working again with Helen Ellis in publicising this book, and with all those in the marketing department of HarperCollins.

David Kynaston and Lara Feigel encouraged me from the outset. After they had read the full manuscript twice they both came up with some extremely helpful and encouraging suggestions, which I took up with gratitude. Lara is a long-term writing companion, and the fact that she thought it was a worthwhile enterprise as we wrote together in Suffolk was a great encouragement to me. David has been a source of help and inspiration since *The Thirties: An Intimate History*, *Wartime: Britain 1939–1945*, and *The Blitz: The British Under Attack*, and he has done the same noble task with this book.

Stella Tillyard made helpful suggestions while Lucy Kynaston came up with a suggestion just at the right time.

I also owe thanks to Jan Crowhurst and Ann Dawney for refreshing my memory about our school days. Thanks too to Jacky Turner, Rebecca Swift and Neil Vickers. Sadly, Henry Horwitz was too unwell to play an active part but encouraged me from across the Atlantic.

Natasha Periyan and Ellie Bass were assiduous researchers. Suki Kaur and Justyna Lizak typed when I couldn't and showed me very many acts of kindness as I worked.

I have learned a great deal from many of the moving autobiographies I have read recently, particularly Lorna Sage's *Bad Blood*, Ferdinand Mount's *Cold Cream*, Jeremy Harding's *Mother Country*, John Lanchester's *Family Romance*, Janet Street-Porter's *Baggage* and Vesna Goldsworthy's *Chernobyl Strawberries*.

I would also like to thank my three children, who have been very supportive throughout a difficult time and never once said: 'Isn't there rather too much about you in this book, Mum?'

Hackney,
March 2017

Picture Credits

Page 1 (top): Juliet Gardiner photographed by Peter Bolton for *TV Times* in 1963. Photograph supplied by the author.

Page 1 (bottom), 3 (top right, bottom left and bottom right), 5 and 8 (top right) courtesy of the author.

Page 2 (top) © William Vandivert / Contributor / Getty Images

Page 2 (bottom) © Bert Kneller / Getty Images

Page 3 (top left) © Haywood Magee / Stringer / Getty Images

Page 4 (top) © IPC Magazines/Picture Post / Contributor / Getty Images

Page 4 (bottom) © Reg Burkett / Stringer / Getty Images

Page 6 (top) © Rolls Press/Popperfoto / Getty Images

Page 6 (middle) © Terrence Spencer / Contributor / Getty Images

Page 6 (bottom) © shepard sherbell / Contributor /Getty Images